A WORLD OF PASTA

A WORLD

Unique Pasta Recipes from

Maria Luisa Scott

OF PASTA

Around the World

and *Jack Denton Scott*

Galahad Books • New York

This edition published by Galahad Books in 1996.

Galahad Books
A division of Budget Book Service, Inc.
386 Park Avenue South
New York, NY 10016

Galahad Books is a registered trademark of Budget Book Service, Inc.

Published by arrangement with McGraw-Hill, Inc.

Library of Congress Catalog Card Number: 82-83226

ISBN: 0-88365-667-1

Printed in the United States of America.

CONTENTS

Cookbooks by Jack Denton Scott:

THE COMPLETE BOOK OF PASTA

FEAST OF FRANCE
(with Antoine Gilly)

THE BEST OF THE PACIFIC COOKBOOK

Cookbooks by Maria Luisa Scott and Jack Denton Scott:

INFORMAL DINNERS FOR EASY ENTERTAINING

COOK LIKE A PEASANT, EAT LIKE A KING

MASTERING MICROWAVE COOKING

A WORLD OF PASTA

FOREWORD

WHEN AMERICANS THINK OF PASTA they usually think of Italy, the country that is synonymous with pasta. But almost every country has its favorite pasta dishes, and our purpose here is to bring some of these lesser-known pasta recipes into the American kitchen.

Why will Americans be interested in these pasta recipes of various peoples? Two compelling reasons: Pasta is inexpensive, and it is one of our favorite foods.

Pasta is so popular in this country that it is estimated we have consumed enough spaghetti alone to stretch to the moon and back 344 times; each of us may eat two-thirds of a mile of it in a lifetime. In the past year Americans consumed approximately 2 billion pounds of pasta, almost 10 pounds per person. It has been estimated that in that single year we mixed our pasta with 435 million gallons of sauce (using one quart of sauce for one pound of pasta), which would fill a lake one mile long, 500 feet wide and about 22 feet deep. That represents about $96 million worth of just commercial pasta sauce and mixes.

According to the National Macaroni Institute, that lake of sauce is rising. Inflation and the growing need to seek nutritious and tasty meals at lower prices pushed pasta purchases up more than 15 percent as this was being written.

Yet, despite our national appetite for pasta, too many of us fail to appreciate the versatility of this flexible food that can stretch a budget and pleasantly fill a belly. We routinely pair pasta with heavy tomato sauce, ignoring the boundless rewards of a food that mates well with everything from anchovies to zucchini.

We also fail to take advantage of the many different sizes, shapes, and types of pasta available to us, prosaically sticking with the familiar forms of spaghetti, macaroni, and noodles. Spaghetti accounts for about 40 percent of U.S. pasta sales, with elbow macaroni a close second at about 35 percent, and noodles nudging in at about 20 percent. Six other varieties fill in the remaining 5 percent

Where possible with our recipes, we have suggested different forms of pasta (mainly Italian, as they are the most imaginative). Most groceries these days carry many varieties, with different names and eye-catching shapes, and you will find them a refreshing change from the usual spaghetti or flat egg noodles. If you can't find the pastas we recommend, however, use whatever you have on hand, as almost any pasta pairs perfectly with any sauce in this book, except, possibly, in the case of some Asian recipes.

Pasta is the generic Italian term for that multitude of products made from semolina and water. Semolina is the golden, sugar-fine flour ground from the heart of durum wheat, the hardest and purest of all wheats. Commercial pasta is made by mixing the proper amounts of semolina and water, shaping the dough, and drying it. Noodles are made in much the same way, except they have eggs added. American pasta also has riboflavin, thiamine, niacin, and iron blended into the dough.

Eaten properly, pasta is *not* a weight builder. One of the world's perfect foods, it is low in fat (1.4 percent for semolina pasta; 4.5 percent for egg noodles), and high in digestibility. Four ounces of cooked pasta contain just 210 calories, about the amount in two small apples. It is an energy-giving carbohydrate, containing more protein (13 percent) than potatoes. Four ounces of cooked pasta has all the vitamins and iron recommended for the U.S. daily allowances for adults. Pasta also rates high in the four groups of the United States Department of Agriculture's Daily Food Guide.

In addition, pasta provides a good distribution of the essential amino acids. With the usual sauces, meat, seafood, fresh vegetables, cheese, eggs, or fruit (tomatoes are fruit), a dish of pasta with sauce makes a perfectly balanced diet, with every amino acid in place.

What genius first put flour and water together to produce this almost perfect food? No one is sure. Historians throw out leads and some facts, but disagree. Some believe the Arabs first used dried pasta to preserve flour and make its cooking easier on their long treks across the deserts. The Arabs are credited with introducing this pasta into Sicily and southern Italy. It is also recorded that the Greeks brought their own pasta, *lasanon*, to southern Italy when it became their Magna Grecia.

But what about Marco Polo? Didn't he introduce pasta into Italy from China, as most of us believe? No. *Ravioli* was being eaten in Rome in 1284 when Marco Polo was a boy, twenty years before he embarked upon his world-famous travels. There is little doubt, however, that Marco Polo did bring back various kinds of pastas from China. He even delivered some curious pasta from Java, which was made from ground breadfruit.

Most Asian pastas do differ from the flour-and-water-and-egg varieties that Western palates favor. In northern China, some noodles are made from wheat flour, but they come in a wide variety of shapes, and are always very long, because long noodles are a symbol of longevity. Chinese noodles are also made from shrimp, rice, corn, peas, beans, or a mung-bean starch paste from which the very thin, transparent cellophane noodles are made. Most other Asian noodles are an adaptation of the Chinese, with many varieties of rice noodles, designated by type and thickness of the strands.

The Japanese are enthusiastic noodlers, using some of the same types as the Chinese, but also creating their own from wheat and buckwheat. Japanese noodles fall into two main categories, *udon*, a large, soft, white noodle, and *soba* which are thin and come in various styles: a gray buckwheat, a curly noodle, a green "tea leaf," and green spinach noodles. There are soba shops all over Japan that specialize in noodles to take out.

If the Oriental or Asian pasta dishes interest you, it shouldn't be difficult to get the genuine noodles in Oriental or specialty shops. Chinese and Japanese cuisine are popular in America, and almost any shop that carries so-called gourmet items will have some of the noodles and condiments. If you have a yen for an Oriental pasta dish and are living in a rural area where all shopping except for meat and potatoes poses a problem, you can use thin American noodles and adjust the recipe accordingly. For example, some of the Asian noodle dishes require that the noodles first be soaked. With American noodles this step is eliminated. Common sense will direct you. If possible, do try to buy the Oriental pastas and experiment. The unusual textures and tastes are well worth trying.

All other pastas are about the same, that is, they are made of flour, water, and/or egg. But some of the methods of making and cooking the pastas differ. We have included techniques for making some of these pastas, and, of course, for cooking them.

In the recipes to come, we have included our favorites gathered from more than a dozen trips around the globe. We have tried to offer variety. Sometimes prejudice rears its pampered head forcing us to favor some countries over others, but withal, we hope that we have offered balance and representation.

One thing is certain: These around-the-world pasta dishes are an adventure in cooking that will eliminate dullness in dining for many a month to come.

I

Making Pasta

*J*UST AS IT ISN'T NECESSARY to grow your own vegetables in order to derive nourishment from them, it isn't required that you make your own pasta. But, just as there is no taste quite like that of a dead-ripe tomato picked from your garden glistening with beads of morning dew, there is no comparison between commercial and homemade pasta. If you do not have the time or the inclination to make pasta, at least try to buy some "fresh" pasta from a shop. In most metropolitan areas, today, there are such shops, and the fresh pasta freezes well, retaining its inimitable taste and flavor. But fresh pasta frozen should not be defrosted before it is cooked. If you do defrost it first, it becomes mushy in the cooking.

For true adventurers of the palate we offer various homemade pasta recipes, including won ton wrappers, Polish kluski, Greek trahana, among others. Perforce, however, we lead off with the basic pasta-making technique of the Italians. It could not be otherwise, for those poets of pasta remain the acknowledged world leaders in the making—and the eating—of pasta.

Pasta Fresca All'Uovo (Fresh Egg Pasta)

Makes about 2 pounds

4 cups of semolina flour
   (or all-purpose white flour)
1½ teaspoons of salt

4 fresh eggs, lightly beaten
2 teaspoons of olive oil
2 teaspoons of warm water

There are good reasons for using semolina flour. It makes tastier pasta and also holds up better in the cooking. But if you can't get it in a specialty shop or an Italian grocery store, don't fret. Common, run-of-the-mill, "all-purpose" flour will do nicely.

Sift the flour onto a pastry board; make a well halfway down into the mound. Into this well sprinkle the salt, pour in the beaten eggs, olive oil, and warm water, adding the liquid gradually to make the dough soft enough to handle. Blend everything well with your hands and form the dough into a ball. Lightly flour the pastry board and knead the ball of dough well, slapping it and pressing down with the heels of your hands until the dough is smooth and pliant. This should take about 15 minutes. Invert a bowl over the dough and let it rest for 15 minutes.

Divide the ball of dough into four pieces. Clean the pastry board and lightly flour it again, and, with a pastry roller, roll each piece of dough into as thin a sheet as you can. Cut the flat sheets of pasta into the widths or shapes desired, place on a clean white cloth and allow to dry for one hour.

One caution, if you use ordinary white flour, your fresh pasta will cook more quickly. Keep your eye on it, and test it often by biting into a piece, otherwise it will emerge from the water too soft and without flavor. Do not use "self-rising" flours, and avoid the new miracle flours, the so-called "instantized" flours. There is no such thing as instant pasta.

The thing to remember in kneading the pasta is: If the flour doesn't hold together as you knead, slowly add small amounts of liquid; or, if the dough is too soft, add more flour—either way, easy does it.

From this dough comes a variety of fresh pastas. The same recipe is used for manicotti, fettuccine, lasagne, cannelloni, tagliatelle, the only difference being in the way the dough is cut. The cutting is done after the dough is rolled and before it is dried. There is a quick and effective way of doing this, which eliminates the laborious process of cutting the pasta strip by strip. After the ball of dough has been divided into three or four pieces and each one rolled into a sheet as thin as you can make it (paper-thin), simply roll up or fold each sheet into a long roll. Then cut the roll crosswise, making strips any width you wish, depending upon the type of pasta you are making. The strips may then be very gently unfolded and cut into the required lengths. You may also lightly toss the cut noodles to unfold them.

To cut manicotti: Cut the sheets of dough into 3-inch squares. Dry on a floured board, covered with a cloth, for one hour.

To cut fettuccine: Cut rolled sheets of dough into ¼-inch strips. Unfold and dry for one hour, covered with a cloth.

To cut lasagne: Cut the dough into strips 2 inches wide, 4- to 6-inches long, depending on how broad you want this noodle. Dry for one hour, covered with a cloth.

To cut cannelloni: The dough for this should not be any thicker than ⅛ inch, even thinner, if possible. Cut the dough into 4- or 4½-inch squares. Dry for one hour, covered with a cloth. Then cook, 5 squares at a time, by popping them into 5 quarts of boiling water for 4 minutes. Remove with a slotted spoon, and drain well on absorbent cloth.

To cut tagliatelle: These are ¾-inch-wide noodles and may be cut from rolled sheets of dough, in the same manner as fettuccine.

Tagliarini are the smallest version of *tagliatelle*, cut ⅛ inch wide.

Pasta Fresca for Ravioli and Tortellini

This dough is handled a little differently. The ingredients below make about 1½ pounds of dough.

3½ cups of semolina flour (or all-purpose flour)
1 teaspoon of salt
2 eggs, lightly beaten

1 tablespoon of olive (or salad) oil and/or 2 tablespoons of warm water

Sift the flour onto a board or marble slab, sprinkle in the salt, make a center well, and add the eggs and oil gently, so that they remain in the well. Now gradually mix well, kneading into a soft dough, slowly adding drops of warm water to soften it, if necessary. Knead from 5 to 10 minutes, long enough to have a smooth elastic dough; cover with pan or bowl for half an hour; then roll out and shape as described below.

To shape ravioli: Reflour the board. Cut the dough into two sections, roll out each section to no more than ⅛ inch thick and cut into 3-inch strips as long as the sheets. Place teaspoons of the desired filling 2½ inches apart on this long strip. Cover with a similar 3-inch-wide strip of dough, pressing the dough firmly around each spoonful of filling. Using a pastry wheel or ravioli cutter, cut into 2- or 3-inch squares, depending upon how large you want the ravioli. They should dry, covered with a cloth, for at least 1½ hours before cooking.

To shape tortellini: This is done somewhat differently from ravioli. Cut the dough into 2-inch circles with a small glass or cooky cutter. Place the filling on the circle, then fold one side of the circle over onto the other to form a half circle. Press the edges of the half circle firmly together, then bend it, seam side out, to form a ring and firmly press together the overlapping points of the original half circle.

A word of caution regarding ravioli, or tortellini, or any of the pastas that are to be filled. After you have rolled the dough and cut it into the proper shapes, place the filling in them immediately, before the dough has dried, as dried dough is difficult to press into form. Place the filled pasta on a clean white cloth, cover with another cloth, and then allow to dry for a half hour.

Pasta Verde (Green Pasta)

Makes about 2 pounds of green noodles

¾ pound of cleaned fresh spinach
4 cups of semolina flour (or all-
purpose flour)

2 eggs, lightly beaten
1 teaspoon of salt

Cook the spinach over low heat without water, well covered, until tender. Drain well, pressing out *all* the liquid. Then force it through a sieve or purée in a food mill or food processor.

Sift the flour onto a board or marble slab. Make a center well, and add the beaten eggs, the salt, and then the spinach, working until the dough is well mixed. Knead for 15 minutes, until it is smooth, adding water if it is too dry or flour if too soft. Separate the smooth ball of dough into three pieces. Then, using a tapered, 2-foot pastry rolling pin, flatten each piece, rolling it and pressing it into extremely thin sheets, ⅛ inch or thinner, if possible. Gently roll the sheets for cutting, as described on page 5, then cut straight across into ⅓- or ¼-inch strips. Unfold the noodles, and dry on a clean white cloth for 1 hour before cooking.

All of the foregoing fresh pastas are made with eggs, thus they are noodles. The following is a recipe for fresh pasta without eggs, in the manner of the commercial dry pasta, except that this pasta will not be hard and dry, and it will be tastier.

Fresh Pasta without Eggs

Makes about 1½ pounds of pasta

3 cups of semolina flour (or all-
purpose flour)
1 teaspoon of salt

2 tablespoons of olive oil
1 cup of warm water

Sift the flour onto a board, make a center well, and add salt, olive oil, and a small amount of water. Slowly mix, bringing flour from around the edges, and kneading together. Add more water as needed; continue kneading until the dough is formed into a smooth ball. Cover dough with a bowl and let it rest for 10 minutes. Now reknead until the dough is smooth and very elastic. Recover with bowl for 15 minutes, then divide dough ball into 3 pieces, and roll into thin, ⅛-inch sheets. Cut strips into desired widths. Dry for 1 hour before cooking

THE FOREGOING RECIPES give the true pasta lover's technique for handling pasta dough. But if you love homemade pasta, yet aren't so fond of the labor involved in rolling it out, then just about any gourmet or specialty food shop has the answer for you: the pasta machine.

There are several types of machines, but we prefer one that first rolls out the dough into the thinnest of sheets, and then, with another attachment, cuts the sheets into widths. A simple adjustment of the dial will give you the proper width for the proper pasta. The machine is a great investment for almost any kind of flat pasta.

Another great time-saver is the food processor, which can make the complete dough in mere seconds. We have tried almost all the commercial processors, and our favorite is the Waring Food Processor, which has a good, powerful motor. Be careful, however, not to overload the machine. Use no more than 2 cups of flour at a time, and make the dough in batches if necessary. For a typical noodle recipe, place 2 eggs, 1 teaspoon salt, 1 teaspoon olive oil, and 4 tablespoons water in the processor and run for 10–15 seconds. Very *slowly* pour remaining cup of flour into mixture and blend until the dough has the proper consistency.

Sonya Murphy's Gnocchi Ricotta

ITALY   Serves 4

1 cup of ricotta
2 cups of flour (semolina or all-
    purpose white flour)

1 tablespoon of salt
1 beaten egg

Mix together the ricotta, flour, salt, and eggs. Turn out on a lightly floured board, knead well. Roll into long fingerlike rolls. Cut into ¼-inch pieces. Roll the pieces into uniform shapes. Using plenty of boiling water, drop in just enough gnocchi to cook without crowding. Cook for about 5 to 7 minutes. Serve with butter and cheese or any sauce. Recipe may be doubled.

Homemade Kluski with Bacon and Cheese

POLAND   Serves 4 to 6

KLUSKI

2¼ cups of sifted all-purpose flour
  2 eggs, beaten

½ teaspoon of salt
3 tablespoons of warm water

Mound the flour on a pastry board and form a well in the center; place the eggs and salt into the well and work into the flour, adding the water as you work the flour, and kneading it into an elastic dough. When little bubbles begin to form, divide the dough into 2 balls. Lightly flour the pastry board and roll each ball into a very thin sheet, no thicker than ⅛ inch. Let the dough stand for 15 minutes, then roll each sheet up as for a jelly roll and cut straight across into the desired width (anywhere from ¼ inch to 1 inch). Shake them out into noodle lengths. Cook in boiling, salted water until *al dente*, drain.

CHEESE AND BACON

1 pound of pot cheese, room   **6 strips of bacon, cooked until crisp,**
   temperature   crumbled (save the bacon fat)

In a bowl, place the cheese, add the hot noodles, and toss. Top with the bacon bits and the bacon fat.

Bombay Potato Noodles

INDIA   Serves 6

We have often had these unique "noodles" served with lamb in the city for which they were named. We once watched a chef cook them, and we have a word of caution: When you add the noodles to the hot fat, the fat will boil up quickly, and if the pot or deep-fryer isn't deep enough it could boil over. So make sure your fryer is a deep one.

2 cups of cooked mashed potatoes   **1 teaspoon of tumeric**
½ cup of chickpea flour   **½ teaspoon of cayenne**
1½ teaspoons of salt   **2 cups of peanut oil**

In a bowl, blend the potatoes, flour, salt, tumeric, and cayenne until the mixture is smooth and thick. Heat the oil in the deep-fryer or pot until a haze forms over it. Using a potato ricer, and working with one-fourth of the potato mixture at a time, squeeze it through the ricer into the hot oil. The noodles should brown in less than a minute. Scoop them out with a slotted spoon and drain on paper towels. Serve them hot with roast meats or cold with cocktails.

Spaetzle

GERMANY   Serves 4 to 6

2½ cups of flour   3 eggs, beaten
1 teaspoon of salt   ½ cup of milk
¼ teaspoon of pepper   2 tablespoons of butter
¼ teaspoon of nutmeg

In a bowl, combine the flour, salt, pepper, and nutmeg. Make a well in the center, pour in the eggs and one-half of the milk. With a fork, or your fingers, mix this into a thick, firm dough that comes away from the sides of the bowl, adding more milk when necessary. Knead the dough on a floured board until smooth. Divide the dough into 3 balls; then, over a pot of salted, boiling water, push the dough through a large-holed colander into the water. You also can roll the dough out on a board to a ⅛-inch thickness and cut into slivers, then slip these into the boiling water. Do not cook too many at a time. When they are cooked (about 5 minutes), they will float. Drain and mix with the butter.

Spaetzle with Croutons

GERMANY   Serves 4 to 6

1 recipe of spaetzle (above) made   1 cup of ¼-inch cubes of day-old
     with 4 tablespoons of minced   bread
     parsley added to the dough   2 tablespoons of minced parsley
4 tablespoons of butter

Cook spaetzle as directed (above), drain and mix with 2 tablespoons of butter. Melt remaining butter in a frypan, add the bread cubes, and cook, tossing until they are coated with butter, and are golden. Mix the spaetzle with the bread cubes and cook 1 minute more. Sprinkle with the parsley.

Spaetzle with Ham

GERMANY   Serves 4 to 6

To the spaetzle dough (page 11) knead in 1 cup of minced cooked ham; cook in boiling water without salt. Drain and toss with 2 tablespoons of butter and ½ cup of grated Gruyère or Swiss cheese.

Spaetzle with Mushrooms

GERMANY   Serves 4 to 6

To one recipe of cooked spaetzle, add ½ pound of thinly-sliced mushrooms that have been sautéed in 3 tablespoons of butter.

Sour Trahana

GREECE

Trahana should be prepared long before you will use them, as the drying period takes several days. Make them in advance and store them in air-tight jars or freeze them. They will hold as long as any dried pasta. Use the trahana in soups.

To make about 3 or 4 cups

2 large eggs   1½ cups farina (or cream of wheat)
1 cup of yogurt   1½ cups of flour
¼ teaspoon of salt

In a bowl with a fork, beat together the eggs, yogurt, and salt, until well mixed. Gradually add equal amounts of farina and flour (you may need more or less than the given amount) until you have a medium-firm dough. Knead the dough on a floured board 5 minutes then divide it into egg-sized pieces. On dish towels or napkins, flatten each as thin as possible with the heel of the hand. Dry thoroughly on one side (it will take overnight in a warm, dry place), then turn the dough and dry on the other side. Crush or break up these flat cakes into rice-sized bits, spread them out, and allow to dry several days, or bake in a very low oven until *thoroughly* dried.

Trahana are also made "sweet" and "sweet-sour." To make the sweet, use milk instead of yogurt. You may need extra salt, farina, and flour for this. To make the sweet-sour use half milk and half yogurt.

Trahana are also available in shops that sell Greek foods.

Hungarian Tarhonya

Serves 6

3 cups of flour
1 teaspoon of salt
3 eggs, beaten
1 egg yolk, beaten

⅓ cup of butter
2 teaspoons of sweet Hungarian
   paprika

In a bowl, sift the flour and salt, blend in the eggs and the egg yolk, working it until a stiff dough is formed. Flour a pastry board and knead the dough for 5 minutes. Cover with a bowl and let it rest for 15 minutes. On the wide opening of a grater, grate the dough, then spread it out on a cloth or baking sheet and let it dry for 24 hours, stirring or turning occasionally. In a frypan, melt the butter, stir in the paprika and over medium heat cook the pasta, stirring and turning until it has an evenly-hued golden color. Cool well and store in airtight jars, or freeze until ready to use. If you freeze (as with all frozen pastas) do not defrost before cooking in boiling salted water, but drop the pasta into the water while still frozen.

Won Ton

CHINA   Makes about 50 wrappers

These thin wrappers of dough are filled with a delicious mixture of meat and/or shellfish, then steamed, dropped into soup or deep-fried. They are a classic Cantonese dish and a favorite of just about everybody.

2 cups of sifted all-purpose flour   **1 egg,** beaten
1 teaspoon of salt   **¼ cup of water**

In a bowl, place the flour and salt (which have been sifted together). Form a well in the center of the flour; into it place the egg and the water and work it into the flour with your fingers, mixing and kneading until a smooth dough develops. Separate the dough into halves. Lightly flour a pastry board, roll out the halves into sheets no thicker than ¹/₁₆ of an inch thick. With a pastry wheel, cut the sheets of dough into 3½-inch squares. Cover the squares with a damp towel while you prepare a filling of your choice. After being filled, they can be dropped into soup or deep-fried as on pages 83 and 84.

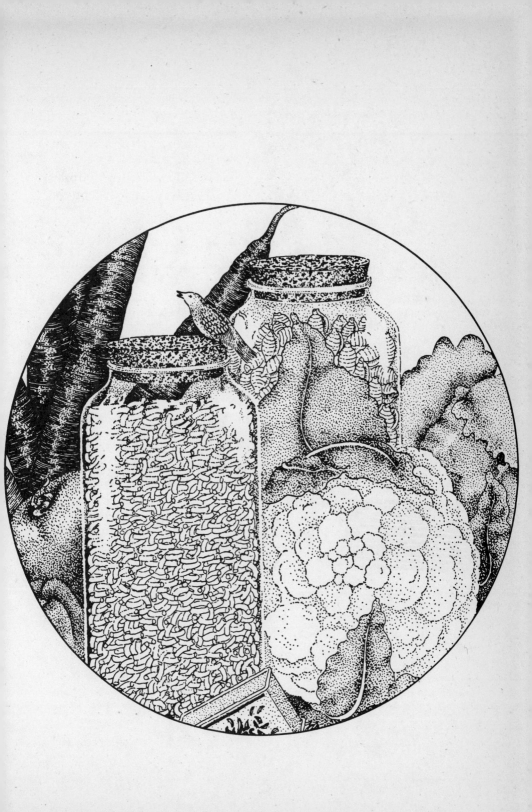

II

Cooking and Eating Pasta

$\mathscr{C}$OOKING PASTA, whether homemade or commercial, is far from the simple act of placing it in hot water and boiling it. We have found that at least six quarts of water should be used for one pound of pasta. It should be a deep pot so the pasta can swim, without the strands or pieces being crowded against one another. Two tablespoons of salt should be added after the water boils and just before the pasta goes in. If the pasta is fresh or large, like lasagna, a tablespoon of olive oil added to the pot will help prevent the pasta from sticking.

Keep the water at the boil as the pasta is added, reducing the heat to medium as the pasta cooks. If cooking strand pasta (spaghetti, vermicelli, etc.) or noodles, stir occasionally with a fork, gently separating the strands as they cook.

We do not believe that pasta can be timed by any chart or any exact number of minutes. Cooking pasta is not precise; it depends upon the size of the pasta and how you like it cooked. The correct way is the Italian way, *al dente*, which simply means "to the tooth." When pasta is done it should be bitable and have no flavor of flour. The Italians like it a little more *al dente* than we do. We prefer it firm, still chewy, but with not *quite* so much of "the bone in it," as the Romans say.

So correct cooking is really rather simple: Use lots of water, watch carefully, give the smaller varieties less time than the larger. Fresh pasta also takes less time than dry commercial pasta, but it requires more sauce, as it is more absorbent.

Mario Borgatti, who has a fresh pasta shop at 632 East 187th Street, the Bronx, in New York City, and makes superb egg noodles and ravioli, gave us the method he uses in cooking his own fresh pasta, which his family has been making for generations. Here are his directions for cooking fresh manicotti and lasagne:

"Manicotti and lasagne require only 1 minute boiling time. (They are boiled only to make them soft enough to work with.) Instead of draining them in a colander, where they may stick to each other, it is advisable to run cold water into the pot (after the one minute boil) and to continue running the cold water until you can fish the lasagne strips or manicotti squares from the water with your hands. Shake off the excess water as you remove the pieces of dough from the pot. It is usually best to place six or eight pieces of dough on a clean cloth to further blot them and then work them into your baking pan. In the case of lasagne, alternate the strips with layers of sauce and filling.

"In preparing manicotti, lay the squares flat on a cloth, placing filling across the center of the dough, not quite reaching the edges on each side. Turn up the edge nearest you, so that it lays on top of the filling. Turn the back edge forward so that it lays on top of, and partially overlaps, the first edge. You now have a 'cannoli-like' tube, which you turn over and place seam side down into a baking pan on a layer of sauce. Continue until the pan has a complete layer of filled manicotti. Spoon more sauce over the top of them and bake.

"Recommended baking time for lasagne and manicotti is 40 minutes in a preheated 375-degree oven. Remove the pan from the oven and allow the pasta to set about ten minutes before serving. Extra sauce may be added to individual portions as desired."

THE OLD PROVEN TRIAL-AND-ERROR TECHNIQUE has taught us that the best way to handle cooked pasta (at least for us, and for many professionals) is the fork-from-the-pot method (*not* Mr. Borgatti's lasagne and manicotti!). Most chefs in Italy use it, too. Too many cookbook authors, however, suggest techniques that can really louse up a dish of pasta. They recommend pouring cooked pasta into a colander, some then even compound the crime and run cold water over it "to stop the cooking" so it won't become too soft. This method literally insures that the pasta will be too soft and gummy.

But back to our fork-from-the-pot way: We keep a large bowl on the back of the stove, not on the heat, but in a position so that it stays warm. In that bowl, we shave a stick, or a quarter of a pound, of butter, for one pound of pasta. Using a fork (there also are spaghetti tongs designed for the purpose), we remove some pasta from the pot, shaking excess water from it, then place it in the warm bowl with the butter. The slight film of water on the pasta helps prevent it from sticking together, as does the butter. When all of the pasta is in the bowl, we mill two liberal turnings of black pepper in, then, using a wooden spoon and fork, gently toss the pasta. Using a cylinder grater, we grate three pieces of Asiago cheese, each about the size of a walnut, into the pasta bowl. Next we add about one-third of the sauce and gently toss the pasta. It is then placed in individual hot dishes or rimmed soup bowls and topped with two generous tablespoons of sauce. More cheese is passed at the table.

Obviously, the fork-from-the-pot method can't be used with all pastas. It is effective with all of the string pastas: spaghetti, linguine, vermicelli, the flat noodles, fettuccine, tagliatelle, etc. But with the shells, or rigatoni, lasagne, tufoli, zita, the elbows, etc., we remove them with a slotted spoon, or a large perforated skimmer. If you must use the colander, do it quickly, get the pasta in and out as fast as possible. Togetherness is not part of pasta cookery, at least not when getting it out of the cooking water. It is our belief that stranded pastas, those without holes or a bore, absorb the sauce only from the outside, and are best mixed to the taste of the diner by himself. Thus, we never oversauce these pastas. But pastas with holes, flutes, and crevices benefit from being well mixed with plenty of sauce before serving, which insures that there will be sauce on the outside and the inside, in the grooved and fluted surfaces.

Pasta dishes that depend upon cream and vegetables should be mixed well before serving, always with an extra couple of spoonfuls of the peas, mushrooms, or whatever the main ingredients are on the top.

If offering pasta as a first course, serve no more than three ounces, a main course four ounces or more, depending upon what is added to the pasta, and the appetites of your family or guests. For example, if serving sausage and spaghetti, you will need less pasta than if you are offering linguine with cream and peas. Roughly, one pound of pasta will serve six people. Most pasta increases its volume by three when cooked.

In most of the recipes, except where different techniques are required (such as Asian, etc.), we suggest what pasta to use in the list of ingredients and state, "cooked al dente, drained." In each case we have not said that the pasta must be hot. We do so now. Unless otherwise stated (as in salads), cook the pasta just before serving or mixing. When we refer to pepper, in every recipe it is black pepper unless otherwise specified.

We also suggest that you carefully read each recipe before going to work on it in your kitchen. It will be helpful to you to do as the professionals do: Assemble ingredients before you begin cooking, and also do the manual chores first, the chopping, slicing, shelling, blanching, precooking various vegetables, etc.

One last note: No respectable cookbook on pasta cookery can be complete without a comment on cheese, one of the major ingredients in most pasta dishes.

The tastiest trio, in our estimation, is Asiago, Parmesan, and Pecorino

Romano, all Italian. Our favorite, Asiago, is a *grana*, or grating type of cheese that originated in the Italian province of Vicenza. There are three kinds, a table cheese, *Asiago di taglio* (slicing cheese) and two grating cheeses, *vecchio* (old) and *stravecchio* (very old). Properly aged, Asiago should be golden, hard, and at least two years old, three is better, before being used with pasta. For our taste, Asiago is nuttier and has more flavor than either Parmesan or Romano. But it is not easy to obtain. The best we have found is produced by the Peter Frigo family, which has been working with Asiago for six generations. An Asiago superior to that made in Italy is made by the Frigos in Wisconsin. Another branch of that family, headed by David Frigo, assisted by his brother Edward, carefully ages that Wisconsin *Asiago* and sells it in New England. If you can't get to their store, you can buy it by mail order, but the order must be for at least five pounds. Their address: Frigo House of Cheese, 46 Summer Street, P.O. Box 446, Torrington, Connecticut 06790.

The best Parmesan, in our opinion, is Parmigiano Reggiano; others that are also very good are Polenghi, Galbani, and Locatelli. Romano is our third choice. If you want to further explore the exciting world of cheese, we can recommend others that we have had and like: Ricotta Siciliano, Caciocavallo, Pepato, Ragusano, Peconino di Tavola.

Beside Italian cheeses there are dozens of others that may be used for pasta, and we have enjoyed finding and using them. It's all part of the fun of being a pasta fan. The Yugoslavs make one called Pago, the Czechoslovakians like their Oschtjepek, the Greeks, Kefalotiri. Sapsago, Sbrinz, Penetelu, Kaskaval are a few other European cheeses that mate well with pasta.

If experimenting with pasta cheeses appeals to you, we suggest hitting the books, then Sherlock Holmesing markets and stores, trying to find the cheeses you've read about. One book we like is *Cheese Varieties and Descriptions*, published by the U.S. Department of Agriculture, Agriculture Handbook No. 54, available from the Government Printing Office, Washington, D.C. 10025. With prices fluctuating these days we can't quote an accurate price for the book, but it is not expensive.

III

Soups

$\mathcal{S}$OUP PUTS THE HEART AT EASE, calms down the violence of hunger, eliminates the tension of the day, and awakens and refines the appetite."

Escoffier, perhaps the greatest of all chefs, uttered these words of wisdom. And he could have added another line. Soup plus *pasta* produces fun. It also produces variety, appeal, and often not only "refines" the appetite but can satisfy it as a complete meal.

Soep, tong, sopa, shchi, zuppa, every country contributes to the poetic litany of soup. But for us, no soup is really complete and satisfying unless it swims with some form of pasta, be it a Syrian yogurt soup with noodles, a Bulgarian romaine lettuce soup with little elbows, or threads of vermicelli floating in a Mexican pea soup.

The fun comes, especially with the youngsters, when you get creative with soup, skipping the ordinary noodles and macaronis, and searching out the almost infinite varieties of pastas that not only give soup inimitable flavor, but style and eye-appeal as well. Choose from Chinese won ton, German spaetzle, Russian pelmeny, Greek trahana through the spectacular Italian display that knows no equal: stelline (little stars), *stivaletti* (little boots), stortini that look like tiny wiggling fish, trifogli (clover leaves), rotelline (tiny wheels), salamini (tiny sausages), semi di mela (apple seeds), orzo ("barley" that looks like rice), and pulcini (little chickens). Thus, with little effort, you can make your pasta soup dishes an advent and an adventure for everyone.

Soup is not only the showcase for pasta, but its soulmate. In addition, soup plus pasta is a pacesetter. When you are offered a first course of pasta swimming in a savory soup, you can almost certainly rest assured that the rest of the dinner will be a delight. People with good taste put pasta in soup.

Avgolemono Soup

GREECE   Serves 6

6 cups of rich chicken broth
½ cup of fides (or vermicelli) or orzo or
    any other small soup pasta
3 eggs, separated
3 tablespoons of lemon juice

Salt and pepper to taste
1 tablespoon of butter
2 tablespoons of minced fresh mint
    (or parsley)

In a large saucepan, heat the broth to a boil. Add the pasta and cook for 5 minutes, or until the pasta is *al dente*. Lower heat so that the soup stops boiling. In a bowl beat the egg whites until stiff. Add the yolks, beat until blended. Beat in the lemon juice a small amount at a time. Gradually stir 1 cup of the hot broth into the egg–lemon-juice mixture. Pour this slowly into the broth, stirring constantly. Cook about 2 minutes, or until the soup thickens. Do not allow it to boil. Season with salt and pepper, stir in the butter, and serve immediately with the fresh mint sprinkled on top.

Pasta Bits and Bean Soup

HUNGARY   Serves 6

1 cup of dried white pea beans, soaked for 4 hours, drained
2 quarts of chicken broth
3 slim carrots, scraped, thinly sliced
1 medium-sized parsnip, scraped and thinly sliced
5 tablespoons of butter
3 medium-sized onions, chopped

1¼ cups of sifted flour
2 teaspoons of salt
½ teaspoon of pepper
1 teaspoon of paprika
1 egg, slightly beaten
2 tablespoons of water
2 knockwurst, poached until tender in water, skinned and sliced

In a large pot, place the beans, broth, carrots, and parsnip. Bring to a boil, then simmer for 1½ hours, until the beans are tender. Scoop out a cup of the beans, press them through a sieve or a food mill, puréeing them. Return the purée to the soup pot. In a saucepan, melt the butter and sauté the onions over medium heat for 8 minutes, or until soft and golden. Sprinkle 2 tablespoons of the flour over the onions, and over low heat, stir until the mixture is smooth. Stir in 1 cup of the bean soup liquid, stirring until well blended. Add this to the soup pot along with the salt, pepper, and paprika. Keep the soup at a simmer.

In a bowl, place the remaining sifted flour. Form a well in the center, add the egg and the water, and work into a smooth dough, adding more water or flour, if necessary, kneading it until it takes form and does not stick to your fingers. On a lightly floured pastry board, roll the dough out into a thin sheet, no more than ⅛ of an inch thick; let it set for 40 minutes. Cut fingernail-size pieces from the dough. Bring the bean soup to a boil and drop the noodle bits into the soup. Reduce to a simmer. Add the slices of knockwurst. The soup is ready when the pasta bits float to the surface.

Tortellini in Beef Broth

ITALY   Serves 6

7 cups of hot beef broth
½ pound of tortellini (a small stuffed
    pasta)

Salt and pepper to taste
2 tablespoons of chopped parsley
Freshly grated Parmesan cheese

Heat the broth to boiling. Add the tortellini. When broth comes to a simmer, lower the heat and cook, uncovered, until the pasta is *al dente*. Taste the broth for seasoning before adding salt and pepper. Sprinkle with parsley and pass the cheese at the table.

Beef Soup with Spaetzle

GERMANY   Serves 6

This is a German classic, always served with their special pasta, spaetzle. Sometimes they first prepare the beef broth by simmering the beef and bones in water until the meat is tender, then removing meat and bones and reducing the broth to give it authority before they cook the vegetables. We are recommending that the cooking begin with beef broth.

1½ pounds of good chuck beef, cut into 1½-inch cubes

2 pounds of beef bones (ask your butcher for marrow bones), cut into 1½-inch pieces

2 quarts of beef broth (canned College Inn is excellent)

2 medium-sized onions, each nailed with a whole clove

2 small bay leaves

½ teaspoon of salt

½ teaspoon of pepper

3 large celery ribs, (scraped and coarsely chopped)

1 small turnip, (scraped and coarsely chopped)

3 medium-sized leeks, only the white part, coarsely chopped

3 medium-sized carrots, scraped and coarsely chopped

2 cups of cooked spaetzle (see recipe for spaetzle, page 11)

In a large pot, place the beef, bones, broth, onions and cloves, bay leaves, salt, and pepper. Bring to a boil, cover, then simmer for 1 hour, skimming off any scum rising to the surface. Remove and discard the onions with cloves and the bay leaves. Remove the marrow bones. Scoop out the marrow and return the marrow to the pot. Add the celery, turnip, leeks, and carrots, then simmer, uncovered, for 40 minutes, or until meat and vegetables are tender. Stir in the spaetzle and cook 3 minutes. Taste for seasoning. Serve in deep soup bowls, with equal portions of beef, vegetables, broth, and pasta.

Belle Paula Soup

FRANCE   Serves 6

6 cups of rich chicken broth

1 cup of capelli d'angelo ("angel's hair," an extremely thin pasta), broken into 1-inch pieces

¾ cup of diced Gruyère cheese

Salt and pepper to taste

2 tablespoons of cognac

2 tablespoons of chopped parsley

In a large saucepan, heat the broth to a simmer. Stir in the pasta and cook 30 seconds, stirring constantly. Add the cheese and stir until it has melted. Season with salt and pepper, and stir in the cognac. Serve with the parsley sprinkled on top of each serving.

Pasta and Broccoli Soup

ALSACE-LORRAINE   Serves 4 to 6

2 tablespoons of butter
6 scallions, all of the white and part of
    the green, coarsely chopped
1 small carrot, scraped and sliced
1 small celery rib, scraped and sliced
3 cups of chicken broth

½ bunch of broccoli (about ¾ pound),
    stems scraped and stems and
    flowerets cut up
Salt and pepper to taste
1 cup of plain cooked pasta (any kind)
½ cup of medium cream
4 to 6 tablespoons of sour cream

In a saucepan, over medium heat, melt the butter. Add scallions, carrot, and celery, and cook 5 minutes or until soft. Pour in the broth, bring to a boil. Add the broccoli, then simmer 10 minutes or until the broccoli is tender (but do not overcook, as it will lose its fresh green color). Season with salt and pepper. When the soup has cooled slightly, pour it into a blender jar with the pasta and blend into a smooth purée. Stop the blender and add the cream, then turn on the blender again for 5 seconds. Taste for seasoning. This soup may be served hot or cold. If served cold, put a tablespoon of sour cream on top of each serving. If you have a food processor you can use it instead of a blender.

Tubettini and Brussels Sprouts Soup

GREAT BRITAIN   Serves 6

3 tablespoons of butter
3 leeks (white part only), cut into
 ¼-inch pieces
1 large potato, finely diced
 Salt and pepper to taste
6 cups of chicken broth

1 pint of Brussels sprouts, coarsely
 chopped
½ cup of tubettini (a small hollow
 soup pasta)
3 tablespoons of chopped parsley
 Freshly grated Double Gloucester
 or any other good grating cheese

In a large pot, heat the butter over medium heat. Add the leeks and potatoes, sprinkle with salt and pepper and sauté for 2 minutes, just to coat
them well. Stir in the broth, bring to a boil, then lower heat and simmer
covered for 5 minutes. Stir in the Brussels sprouts, simmer 10 minutes or
until the vegetables are just about cooked. Add the tubettini and cook, uncovered, 5 minutes or until *al dente*. Taste for seasoning. Serve sprinkled with
parsley and pass the cheese at the table.

Acini di Pepe, Carrot, and Potato Soup

NORWAY   Serves 6 to 8

1 tablespoon of cooking oil
2 tablespoons of butter
1 medium-sized onion, minced
1 large carrot, scraped and cut into
 ¼-inch dices
2 medium-sized potatoes, cut into
 ½-inch dices
½ cup of chopped tender celery leaves

Salt and pepper to taste
Pinch of dried marjoram
6 cups of hot rich beef broth
½ cup of acini di pepe ("peppercorns"), or any very small soup
 pasta
2 tablespoons of chopped chervil
 or parsley

In a large pot, heat the oil and butter. Stir in the onion, carrot, potatoes, and celery leaves. Sprinkle lightly with salt and pepper. Add the marjoram and simmer, covered, 5 minutes. Add the broth and simmer, uncovered, for 10 minutes or until the vegetables are just slightly underdone. Add the pasta, cook 5 minutes, or until the pasta is *al dente*. Taste for seasoning. Sprinkle with chervil or parsley.

Anellini, Cream, and Chicken Soup

SWITZERLAND   Serves 6

3 cups of light cream
3 cups of rich chicken broth
½ cup of anellini (small pasta "rings")
1 whole egg and 1 egg yolk, well
    beaten

Pinch of nutmeg
Salt and pepper to taste
1 tablespoon of butter

In a large saucepan, bring the cream and broth to a simmer. Add the pasta and cook until *al dente*. Add ½ cup of the hot soup liquid to the beaten egg and egg yolk, mixing well. Remove the saucepan from the heat. Add the egg mixture, nutmeg, salt, pepper, and butter. Stir until the butter has melted.

Soup-and-Chicken Dinner in One

GREECE   Serves 6

1 **five-pound chicken**
2 **quarts of water**
1 **celery rib,** cut in half
1 **large yellow onion,** cut in half
1 **carrot,** cut in half
1 **teaspoon of salt**
½ **teaspoon of pepper**
12 **small potatoes,** steamed

2 **garlic cloves,** put through the
   garlic press
2 **tablespoons of olive oil**
½ **teaspoon of dry oregano**
1 **cup of kritharaki** (or orzo) or other
   small pasta
2 **eggs,** separated
Juice of 1 lemon

Place the chicken in a soup pot, cover it with water, add the celery, onion, carrot, salt, and pepper. Poach at a simmer for 1 hour with the cover propped with a wooden spoon, skimming off any scum that forms. Take the chicken from the stock (reserve the stock) and place it in a roasting pan. Blend the garlic, olive oil, and oregano well; with your hands rub this over the chicken. Pour about ⅓ cup of the stock into the roasting pan. Arrange the potatoes around the bird; cook in a preheated 400-degree oven 40 minutes, or until the bird is brown and tender and the potatoes are brown.

Strain the chicken stock and discard the vegetables. Bring 5 cups of the stock to a boil, and cook the pasta in it until *al dente*. Do not overcook. In a bowl, beat the egg whites until stiff. Add the yolks, beat until blended, then slowly add and beat in the lemon juice. Gradually stir in 1 cup of the hot stock (from the pasta pot). Return this mixture to the pasta pot, stirring rapidly until well mixed. Serve the pasta soup first, then follow with the chicken, potatoes, and a hearty Greek salad.

Japanese Chicken Noodle Soup

JAPAN   Serves 6

The Japanese are known throughout the East as the "poets of the palate" because of their custom of making all their food offerings appeal to the eye.

8 cups of rich but clear chicken broth
1 large whole chicken breast
½ teaspoon of salt
½ teaspoon of Japanese pepper
  (sansho)

4 ounces of dry bean-thread noodles,
  soaked in warm water 10
  minutes, drained
6 strips of dry seaweed (wakame)
  soaked in warm water 10
  minutes, drained

In a pot, place the chicken broth, bring to a boil, reduce to a simmer. Add the chicken breast and poach, uncovered, for 35 minutes, or until the breast is tender. Remove any scum that rises to the surface while poaching the chicken. Cool the breast, remove the meat from the bones and shred it. Sprinkle with salt and pepper. In 6 soup bowls, arrange equal portions of chicken, noodles, and 1 strip of seaweed. Pour in the steaming hot broth and garnish with anything green that strikes your fancy and brings out the poet in you. Finally minced green tails of scallions, young parsley leaves, and watercress, all are excellent.

Ditalini, Chicken, and Romaine Lettuce Soup

BULGARIA   Serves 6 to 8

1 whole chicken breast
4 chicken backs
4 chicken wings
1 carrot, cut up
1 cup celery leaves
1 large onion cut into halves with
    a clove stuck into one of the
    halves
1 one-pound can of tomatoes
    (tomatoes must be chopped)

Pinch of marjoram
2 teaspoons of salt
½ teaspoon of pepper
3 quarts of water
1 cup of ditalini (small, short
    macaroni)
2 cups (packed), coarsely broken up
    Romaine lettuce

In a large pot place everything but the ditalini and lettuce. Bring to a boil and lower heat and simmer with top ajar (prop lid with a wooden spoon laid across the top of the pot) for 45 minutes or until the chicken is tender. Remove the chicken and reserve the breast. Continue to simmer the stock, uncovered, until you have about 6 cups of stock. Meanwhile, remove the meat from the breast bones and cut into ½-inch cubes. Strain the stock, pushing the vegetables through the strainer. Return the stock to the pot, bring to a boil, stir in the ditalini, lower heat, and simmer 5 minutes or until ditalini is barely *al dente*. Stir in the lettuce and cook 3 minutes or until lettuce and pasta are cooked. Taste for seasoning. Add the cut-up chicken during the last 5 minutes of the cooking.

Capellini and Chickpea Soup (Fideo y Garbanzos Sopa)

MEXICO   Serves 4 to 6

¾ cup of fatback (sometimes labeled in markets as "Pork for Beans"), cut into ½-inch cubes
6 ounces of capellini (a very fine string pasta), broken into small pieces
2 medium-sized onions, chopped
1 garlic clove, minced

4 cups of hot chicken broth
1 large, ripe tomato, peeled, seeded, and finely chopped
1 cup of cooked, drained chickpeas, mashed
Salt and pepper to taste
2 tablespoons of chopped fresh cilantro (coriander) or parsley

In a large saucepan render the fatback golden and crisp. Remove with a slotted spoon and reserve. Pour off all but 2 tablespoons of fat, reserving the remaining fat. Add the capellini and sauté until golden. Remove with a slotted spoon and reserve. Add the onions and garlic to the same pan (adding more of the fat if necessary) and sauté until soft. Add the chicken broth and tomato. Simmer 20 minutes. Stir in the chickpeas and capellini, simmer 2 minutes or until the capellini is *al dente*. Season with salt and pepper. Serve with crisp bits of fatback and cilantro (or parsley) sprinkled over the top.

Macaroni and Chili Soup (a Mexican "dry" soup)

                                                  Serves 4 to 6

2 tablespoons of lard or butter
1 medium-sized onion, chopped
2 sweet red or green chili peppers, seeded, inner white ribs removed and chopped
½ teaspoon of salt

Dash of tabasco
2 cups of Filetto Sauce (see page 206)
2 cups of elbow macaroni, cooked *al dente*, drained
½ cup of a freshly grated sharp cheese of your choice

In a large saucepan heat the lard or butter and sauté the onion and chili peppers until soft. Add the salt, tabasco sauce, and tomato sauce and simmer 3 minutes. Taste for seasoning. Mix in the macaroni, then spoon the mixture into a buttered baking dish. Sprinkle the cheese on top and bake in a preheated 375-degree oven for 20 minutes or until the cheese is golden and the sauce bubbles.

Pasta and Creole Crabmeat Soup

UNITED STATES   Serves 6 to 8

3 tablespoons of butter
2 medium-sized onions, chopped
3 tablespoons of flour
1 small bay leaf
6 fresh, ripe tomatoes, skinned, seeded, and chopped
2 cups of crabmeat, flaked
1½ teaspoons of salt

½ teaspoon of pepper
9 cups of chicken broth
2 small orka, thinly sliced
1 tablespoon of chili powder
12 ounces of funghini (small pasta "mushrooms"), or any small soup pasta, cooked *al dente*, drained

In a pot, melt the butter and cook the onions over medium heat until soft. Stir in the flour and cook for 8 minutes, or until brown. Add the bay leaf, tomatoes, and crabmeat. Cook, covered, over low heat for 10 minutes. Add the salt, pepper, and chicken broth. Bring to a boil, then reduce to a simmer, and cook, covered, 25 minutes. Stir in the okra and chili powder and cook 8 minutes. Taste for seasoning. Place the cooked pasta in soup bowls; pour in the hot soup.

Escarole and Noodle Soup

CHINA   Serves 6

6 cups of rich chicken broth (home-
    made is best)
1 large head of escarole
2 tablespoons of peanut oil
½ pound of shredded lean pork

1 cup of cooked, drained cellophane
    noodles (or another very fine
    noodle)
2 tablespoons of soy sauce
    Salt to taste

Heat the broth in a large saucepan. Separate, trim, wash, and dry the
leaves of the escarole. Coarsely chop the leaves and stir them into the hot
broth. Cover and simmer 5 minutes. Heat the oil in a frypan, add the pork
and sauté, stirring, for 7 minutes or until the strips are browned. Remove
the pork and add it to the saucepan with the broth and escarole. Stir in the
cellophane noodles and soy sauce. Taste for seasoning. Simmer for 2 minutes
and serve.

Hearty Fish Soup with Garlic Sauce

GREECE   Serves 6 to 8

¼ cup of olive oil
1 large white onion, coarsely
    chopped
2 large celery ribs, scraped and cut
    into ¼-inch cubes
1 medium-sized carrot, scraped and
    cut into ¼-inch cubes
3 leeks (white part and some of the
    green), cut into ¼-inch pieces

3 garlic cloves, minced
1 bay leaf
1 cup of chopped parsley
4 cups of water
2 cups of dry white wine
6 large ripe tomatoes, peeled, seeded,
    finely chopped or a one-pound,
    twelve-ounce can of tomatoes,
    broken up

2 seven-ounce cans of minced clams,
   drained, save the liquid
½ pound of fides (or vermicelli), or
   any other small soup pasta

2 pounds of fish fillets (cod, halibut,
   haddock, or other fresh white
   fish), cut into large pieces
Salt and pepper to taste
Flour
Juice of 1 lemon

Heat the olive oil in a large soup pot. Add the onion, celery, carrot, leeks, and garlic, and sauté 5 minutes. Add the bay leaf, parsley, water, wine, tomatoes, and the liquid from the canned clams. Bring to a boil, lower heat, simmer uncovered 30 minutes. Add the pasta. Cook for 5 minutes, or until the pasta is still very resistant to the bite. (For convenience, the term "very *al dente*" will be used to denote very firm, very lightly-cooked pasta.) Season the fillets and roll them in flour. Wrap the fish loosely in cheesecloth and tie the ends. Add this to the soup pot and cook 20 minutes, uncovered, until tender, or until the fish can be flaked with a fork. Unwrap the fish and flake it. Add the fish, clams, and lemon juice to the pot. Heat until the liquid starts to simmer. Taste for seasoning and serve with a bowl of Garlic Sauce and crusty bread.

GARLIC SAUCE   For about 3 cups

5 garlic cloves, put through a garlic
   press
2 cups of mashed potatoes

1 cup of olive oil
½ cup of vinegar
Salt and pepper to taste

Place the garlic and potatoes in a blender or food processor and blend until smooth. Add olive oil and vinegar alternately, small amounts at a time, and blend after each addition until all has been added and the sauce is smooth. Season to taste.

Green Pea Soup with Stelline

FRANCE   Serves 6 to 8

1 tablespoon of olive oil
2 tablespoons of butter
4 large leeks, white part only, cut in
    half lengthwise, washed well,
    and cut into thin slices
  Salt and pepper
6 cups of rich, hot chicken broth

1 ten-ounce package of frozen tiny
    peas, defrosted
½ teaspoon of sugar
  Pinch of thyme
¾ cup of stellini (small "stars")
2 tablespoons of chopped parsley

In a large pot, heat the oil and butter, stir in the leeks. Sprinkle lightly with salt and pepper. Cook, covered, 5 minutes or until the leeks are soft. Add the broth, peas, sugar, and thyme. Simmer, uncovered, 10 minutes. Stir in the pasta and cook 5 minutes or until cooked *al dente*. Taste for seasoning. Serve with parsley sprinkled over the top.

Tomato Soup with Lamb Dumplings

LEBANON   Serves 6 to 8

1 recipe for basic dough for noodles, ravioli, etc. (page 6)

FILLING FOR DUMPLINGS

Prepare the filling first so the dough will not dry out.

1 tablespoon of butter
1 medium-sized onion, minced
1 pound of lean ground lamb
3 tablespoons of minced fresh mint,
    or 1 tablespoon dried

2 teaspoons of minced sultana raisins
½ teaspoon of cumin
  Salt and pepper to taste

In a frypan over medium heat, melt the butter. Sauté the onion until soft. Add the lamb and sauté until it loses its pink color. Remove from the heat. Stir in the mint, raisins, cumin, salt, and pepper; mix well. Spoon this mixture into a strainer over a bowl to drain, saving the drippings.

Cut the dough into 1½-inch squares. Place a small teaspoonful of the drained lamb mixture in one corner, so pasta can be folded over into a triangle and sealed. Moisten edges of the squares with a little water. Bring the corners together and press firmly to seal. Continue this until all the pasta or filling is used. Cook the dumplings in the Tomato Broth.

TOMATO BROTH

3 tablespoons of butter
2 garlic cloves, minced
3 tablespoons of chopped fresh basil,
  or 1 tablespoon dried
6 ripe tomatoes, skinned, seeded,
  and finely chopped

Salt and pepper to taste
2 quarts of beef or chicken broth
Drippings saved from cooking the
  filling
Yogurt

In a frypan over medium heat, melt the butter. Add the garlic and sauté 1 minute. Stir in the basil, sauté 1 minute. Add the tomatoes, salt and pepper, and simmer 15 minutes, uncovered.

Meanwhile, in a large pot, bring the broth to a boil. Add the contents of the tomato-frypan and the drippings to it. Bring mixture to a boil. Reduce heat and add the dumplings to the broth, cooking them a few at a time. Do not crowd them. Simmer until tender, about 10 minutes, then remove the cooked dumplings from the broth and keep them warm in a low oven. Repeat this procedure until all the dumplings are cooked. Taste soup for seasoning. Serve dumplings in a soup bowl with a ladle of the soup added and topped with a dollop of yogurt.

Lamb and Vegetable Soup

GREECE   Serves 6 to 8

THE STOCK

2 **pounds of lean lamb** (shanks,   2 **celery ribs,** quartered
   breast, neck) cut into small   1 **garlic clove,** mashed
   bite-sized pieces   1 **bay leaf**
3 **quarts of cold water**   ½ **teaspoon of oregano**
1 **large onion,** quartered   1 **teaspoon of salt**
2 **carrots,** quartered   ½ **teaspoon of pepper**

Place all of the ingredients in a large soup pot. Bring to a boil, skim off any scum that forms. Lower heat and simmer (with pot cover propped up with a wooden spoon) for 1½ to 2 hours, or until the lamb is tender. Remove the meat with a slotted spoon and set aside. Taste the stock. If it does not have enough flavor, continue to simmer to reduce it, adding more seasoning if necessary. Strain the stock, discard the vegetables, and refrigerate the stock until the fat on top sets, then remove the fat.

THE SOUP

1 **medium-sized onion,** chopped   2 **tablespoons of olive oil**
1 **carrot,** scraped and cut into ¼-inch ½ **cup of tomato purée**
   dices   1 **cup of fides** (or vermicelli) or orzo
1 **large celery rib,** scraped and cut   **Salt and pepper to taste**
   into ¼-inch dices   2 **tablespoons of chopped parsley**

In a large saucepan, over medium heat, cook the onion, carrot, and celery in the olive oil for 4 minutes, stirring well so the vegetables are coated with the oil. Sprinkle lightly with salt and pepper. Stir in the tomato purée. Pour in the lamb stock. Bring to a simmer and cook about 10 minutes, or until the vegetables are barely tender. Stir in the pasta, cook 5 minutes or until *al dente*. Taste for seasoning. Stir in the reserved lamb pieces and cook just until the meat is heated through. Serve with the parsley sprinkled on top.

Orzo, Lamb, and Lentil Soup

ALGERIA   Serves 6

2 tablespoons of olive oil
1 pound of lean lamb cut into ½- to
    ¾-inch cubes
    Salt and pepper to taste
8 cups of chicken broth
1 cup of lentils, rinsed, soaked in
    water to cover for 2 hours, then
    drained
1 medium-sized onion, minced

1 small carrot, scraped, and finely
    chopped
1 garlic clove, minced
2 tablespoons of butter
¼ teaspoon of cumin
¼ teaspoon of cinnamon
1 cup of orzo (a pasta that looks like
    rice, but the name means
    "barley")

In a large saucepan, heat the oil. Add the lamb cubes, season with salt and pepper, and then brown them. Add one-half of the broth, cover, and simmer 30 minutes or until the lamb is tender but still slightly underdone. Stir in the lentils and the remaining broth and simmer 15 minutes. Meanwhile sauté the onion, carrot, and garlic in the butter until soft; sprinkle with the cumin and cinnamon; add them and the orzo to the pot. Cover, keeping lid ajar (prop it with a wooden spoon laid across the pot) and simmer 10 minutes or until the lamb and lentils are cooked and the pasta is *al dente*. Taste for seasoning. This is a hearty, tasty soup.

Sopa de Macarron Albondigas   (Soup of Macaroni Meatballs)

MEXICO   Serves 6

½ pound of ground beef
¼ pound of ground lean pork
½ cup of cooked, mashed macaroni
1 garlic clove, minced
1 egg, beaten
½ teaspoon of salt
½ teaspoon of pepper
½ teaspoon of cumin

1 tablespoon of lard (or butter)
1 tablespoon of olive oil
3 scallions, including some of the
    green part, chopped
½ cup of tomato purée
6 cups of rich beef broth
1 tablespoon of chopped coriander or
    parsley

In a bowl combine and mix well the beef, pork, macaroni, garlic, egg, salt, pepper, and cumin. Shape into small meatballs about ½-inch in diameter. In a large saucepan, over medium heat, heat the lard (or butter) and oil, and very lightly but evenly brown the meatballs. Remove the meatballs and pour off all but 1 tablespoon of fat. Add the scallions and cook until soft. Stir in the tomato purée and the broth and simmer, covered, 10 minutes. Return the meatballs to the pot and simmer uncovered, ½ hour. Sprinkle with coriander or parsley.

Mexican Vermicelli Soup

Serves 6 to 8

2 tablespoons of lard
8 ounces of vermicelli, broken into
    2-inch pieces
6 tablespoons of tomato purée
1 teaspoon of onion juice

2 quarts of beef broth
    Salt and pepper to taste
4 tablespoons of grated Asiago or
    Parmesan cheese

In a large pot, heat the lard and brown the vermicelli. Remove the pasta with a slotted spoon, leaving the fat in the pan. Add the tomato purée and onion juice and simmer for 2 minutes. Add the vermicelli and beef broth. Season to taste with salt and pepper, bring to a boil, reduce to a simmer, and cook, uncovered, for 15 minutes, or until the pasta is cooked *al dente*. Serve with the cheese sprinkled on top.

Mussel Soup with Macaroni (Sopa de Almejas y Macarrones)

SPAIN   Serves 6

24 mussels, at least, in their shells
2 tablespoons of olive oil
1 tablespoon of butter
3 cups of clam juice
2 cups of chicken broth
½ cup of dry white wine

¼ cup of tomato purée
1 cup of ditalini (small, short macaroni)
Pepper to taste
2 tablespoons of chopped parsley

Thoroughly scrub the mussels, then dry them. Heat the oil and butter in a saucepan large enough to hold all the ingredients. Add the mussels, and continue to heat until they open. When the shells open, remove the mussels. Pour their liquid back into the saucepan. Reserve the mussels and discard their shells. Pour in the clam juice, chicken broth, wine, and tomato purée. Bring to a boil, add the macaroni and cook 5 minutes. Add the mussels and pepper and cook until the macaroni is *al dente*. Taste for seasoning. Serve sprinkled with the parsley.

Niçoise Vegetable Soup with Garlic and Basil

FRANCE   Serves 8 to 10

This soup, flavored with pistou, a Provence version of the Genoese pesto (which is also included in this book), was originally an early summer dish but now, with frozen vegetables and dried basil, it can be prepared anytime. However, it is infinitely better made with fresh vegetables and fresh basil. The soup should have tomatoes, green beans, and potatoes, but other vegetables, such as peas and green or red peppers, can be added. Use any amount of the latter, as you like.

3 medium-sized onions, chopped
3 tablespoons of olive oil
2 medium-sized tomatoes, peeled, seeded, and chopped
2 medium-sized potatoes, diced
1 large celery rib, scraped and diced
2 medium-sized carrots, scraped and diced
3 quarts of water

1 teaspoon of salt
½ teaspoon of pepper
1 cup of cooked navy beans
1 cup of green string beans, diced
2 small zucchini, cut into ¼-inch-thick slices
1 cup of spagetti or spaghettini, broken up
Pinch of saffron

In a large, heavy pot, over medium heat, cook the onions in the oil until they are soft. Add the tomatoes, simmer for 5 minutes. Add the potatoes, celery, carrots, water, salt, and pepper. Bring to a boil over high heat then reduce heat and simmer, uncovered, for 15 minutes. Stir in the navy beans, string beans, zucchini, the pasta, and the saffron. Simmer for 10 minutes or until the vegetables are tender and the pasta is *al dente*. Taste for seasoning.

While the soup is cooking, prepare:

THE PISTOU

3 large garlic cloves, minced
½ cup of finely chopped fresh basil or
   3 tablespoons of dried basil.
¼ cup of tomato purée

1 cup of freshly grated Parmesan
   cheese
¼ cup of olive oil

Pound the garlic and basil together in a mortar (or chop in a food processor). Add the tomato purée and one-half of the cheese and blend. Add the oil, one tablespoonful at a time, mixing well after each tablespoon has been added. When ready to serve, pour the pistou into a tureen, stir in a cup of the soup liquid, then stir in the remaining soup. Serve with hot crusty bread and the remaining cheese.

Oxtail (or Beef Shin) Soup with Orzo

PUERTO RICO
                               Serves 6

2 quarts of beef broth (College Inn
   is excellent)
2 pounds of oxtails (or beef shins),
   cut into 2-inch pieces
2 tomatoes, skinned and quartered
2 onions, quartered
3 ears of corn, cut off and use the
   kernels
2 small green peppers, seeded and
   quartered

3 small garlic cloves
⅓ cup of coriander (or parsley) leaves
2 medium-sized zucchini, peeled and
   cut into 1-inch pieces
½ cup of tomato purée
½ teaspoon of salt
½ teaspoon of pepper
3 ounces of orzo (a rice-shaped pasta)

In a large pot, place the beef broth, oxtails (or beef shins), tomatoes, onions, corn, peppers, garlic, coriander, leaves, and zucchini. Bring to a boil, cover and simmer for 1 hour, or until the oxtails and vegetables are fork-tender. With a skimmer, or a slotted spoon, take the vegetables from the pot and place into a blender or food processor. Add ¾ cup of the stock from the pot and blend at high speed for 30 seconds. Pour the vegetable purée back into the pot. Stir in the tomato purée, salt, and pepper; bring to a boil and add the orzo. Cook, over medium heat, uncovered, stirring, for 5 minutes, or until the pasta is still a trifle chewy. The meat will have cooked from the bones. Remove and cut up the meat. Discard the bones. Taste for seasoning. Serve in deep soup bowls with liberal portions of the tender meat.

German Spaetzle and Potato Soup

Serves 8 to 10

3 tablespoons of butter
3 medium-sized potatoes, peeled and cut into ½-inch cubes
2 leeks, white part only (or 1 medium-sized onion), chopped
1 celery rib, scraped and chopped

Salt and pepper
8 cups of beef broth
½ recipe (about 2 cups) of cooked spaetzle (see page 11)
2 cups of diced cooked beef or lamb

In a large heavy pot, melt the butter, add the potatoes, leeks, and celery, sprinkle lightly with salt and pepper, and cook until the celery is soft. Add the broth and simmer for 20 minutes, or until the potatoes are tender. Taste for seasoning. Stir in the spaetzle and the meat; simmer just long enough to heat the spaetzle and the meat.

Vermicelli and Sausage Soup (a Mexican "dry" soup)

Serves 6

Mexicans serve what are called "dry" and "wet" soups. In the "dry" soups most of the liquid is absorbed by the pasta, rice, or tortillas that are used, and don't resemble soups with a noticeable amount of liquid as most countries serve them. Mexicans call soups with liquid "wet" soups.

2 tablespoons of lard (or butter)
3 scallions, including some of the green part, chopped
1 garlic clove, minced
¾ cup of sausage meat (chorizos or Italian)
1 teaspoon of chili powder
3 medium-sized, ripe tomatoes, peeled, seeded, and chopped

or 1 one-pound can of tomatoes, chopped
3 cups of rich chicken broth
½ teaspoon of salt
½ teaspoon of pepper
8 ounces of vermicelli, broken into 1-inch pieces
½ cup of a grated, sharp cheese of your choice

Use a pot that can go from the top of the stove to the broiler. Place it over medium heat and melt the lard (or butter) in it. Add the scallions and garlic and sauté them until soft. Add the sausage meat and chili powder and cook for 10 minutes, breaking the sausage up with a fork. Add the tomatoes and simmer 10 minutes or until the watery part has cooked off. Add the broth, salt, and pepper. Heat to a boil. Stir in the vermicelli; lower heat and cook, uncovered, until all the liquid has been absorbed (if the liquid is absorbed before the pasta is *al dente*, add a small amount of hot broth). Taste for seasoning. Sprinkle the top with the cheese and place under the broiler until the cheese has melted and is golden.

Sour Shrimp Noodle Soup

CHINA   Serves 4 to 6

4 tablespoons of dried shrimp
½ cup of dried black mushrooms
¼ cup of wood-ear fungus
6 cups of chicken broth
2 tablespoons of soy sauce
1 teaspoon of salt

1 cup of dried shrimp noodles
½ cup of white vinegar
2 tablespoons of cornstarch ⎤
2 tablespoons of water   ⎦ blended
3 small eggs, beaten

In separate cups, place the dried shrimp, the mushrooms, and the fungus; cover with boiling water and let set for 15 minutes. Drain all well and shred the mushrooms and the fungus. In a pot, place the chicken broth, shrimp, shredded mushrooms, fungus, soy sauce, and salt. Bring to a boil, stir in the noodles, reduce heat to a simmer and cook for 8 minutes, or until the noodles are tender. Stir the vinegar, the blended cornstarch and water, and the eggs into the pot. Cook, stirring, for 2 minutes or until the soup starts to thicken. Taste for seasoning.

German Spaetzle-Green Split Pea Soup

                                                   Serves 6 to 8

3 slices of lean bacon, chopped
2 medium-sized onions, chopped
1 small celery rib, scraped and
   chopped
1 small carrot, scraped and chopped
   Pepper to taste
6 cups of chicken broth
1 pound of green split peas, rinsed
   and soaked in water to cover for
   2 hours, drained

2 cups of ½-inch cubes of cooked
   meat or fowl
½ recipe (about 2 cups) of cooked
   spaetzle (page 11)
3 frankfurters, cut into ⅛-inch-thick
   slices
2 tablespoons of chopped parsley
⅓ cup of white vinegar

In a large heavy pot, cook the bacon 1 minute. Add the onions, celery, carrot, and pepper. Cook until the vegetables are soft. Pour in the broth, stir in the peas, and simmer, covered, for 45 minutes, or until the peas are just about cooked. Add the meat or fowl and simmer, covered, 10 minutes. Add the spaetzle and frankfurters, and simmer, uncovered, 5 minutes, or until they are heated through. Taste for seasoning. Just before serving, stir in the parsley and vinegar.

Sopa de Macarron y Espinacas (Macaroni and Spinach Soup)

MEXICO   Serves 6

1 tablespoon of lard (or butter)
1 small onion, minced
1 small garlic clove, minced
½ cup of tomato purée
6 cups of rich chicken broth
2 cups of broken-up perciatelli (a
     hollow pasta larger than
     spaghetti) cooked very *al dente*,
     drained

1 cup (packed) coarsely-chopped raw
     spinach
Salt and pepper to taste
¼ teaspoon of nutmeg
Freshly grated Asiago cheese

In a large saucepan, over medium heat, melt the lard (or butter). Add the onion and garlic and cook until they are soft. Add the tomato purée and broth and simmer 5 minutes. Add the cooked pasta, spinach, salt, pepper, and nutmeg. Simmer for 10 minutes or until the pasta and the spinach are tender. Taste for seasoning. Serve with the cheese.

Sposata (Noodle Soup Married to Cheese, Egg Yolk, and Cream)

ITALY   Serves 6 to 8

6 cups of boiling chicken broth
¼ pound of capellini (a very fine
    string pasta), broken up
4 tablespoons of sweet butter, soft
    but not melted

1 cup of grated Asiago or Parmesan
    cheese
3 egg yolks
    Pinch of nutmeg
    Salt and white pepper to taste
1 cup of heavy cream

Add the capellini to the broth and cook over medium heat until *al dente* (it will take only a few seconds). In a bowl, blend the butter, cheese, egg yolks, nutmeg, salt, and pepper. Add the cream, a small amount at a time, mixing well. Add 4 tablespoons of the hot broth to this mixture, stirring after each spoonful has been added, then vigorously stir contents of the bowl into the broth and capellini pot. Heat to a simmer; do not boil. Serve immediately.

Tomato Soup with Semi di Melone

LEBANON   Serves 6

2 tablespoons of butter
1 tablespoon of olive oil
1 medium-sized onion, sliced
1 garlic clove, minced
    Salt and pepper to taste
4 medium-sized, ripe tomatoes,
    peeled, seeded, and finely
    chopped or 1 one-pound can of
    tomatoes, finely chopped

2 cups of hot water
3 cups of hot beef broth
2 cups (packed) shredded escarole
¾ cup of semi di melone ("melon
    seeds") pasta
    Juice of ½ lemon
1 tablespoon of minced fresh mint
    leaves or 1 teaspoon of dried
    mint, crushed

In a large saucepan, over medium heat, heat the butter and oil. Add the onion and garlic. Season lightly with salt and pepper and sauté until soft. Stir in the tomatoes and simmer 5 minutes, mashing them with a wooden spoon. Add the water, broth, and escarole, and simmer 20 minutes. Stir in the pasta, and cook 5 minutes or until it is *al dente*. Stir in the lemon juice and mint leaves. Simmer for 1 minute. Taste for seasoning.

French Tomato Soup

Serves 6

2 tablespoons of butter
1 medium-sized white onion, minced
4 ripe tomatoes, peeled, seeded, and chopped
Salt and pepper to taste

3 cups of chicken broth
2 cups of water
1 cup of capelli d'angelo (a very fine pasta), broken up

Heat the butter in a large, heavy saucepan. Add the onion and cook until it is soft. Add the tomatoes, salt, pepper, chicken broth, and water. Bring to a boil, reduce heat, and simmer, uncovered, for 30 minutes. Strain the soup, pushing the tomato and onion through the strainer. Bring the liquid to a boil, add the pasta, and cook no more than 1 minute or until it is *al dente* (which will be almost immediately).

Tomato Soup with Trahana

GREECE   Serves 6

1 small white onion, chopped
1 large celery rib, scraped and
    chopped
3 tablespoons of olive oil
4 ripe tomatoes, peeled, seeded, and
    chopped or a one-pound can of
    tomatoes, chopped
4 cups of rich chicken broth

1 bay leaf
½ teaspoon of dry basil
1 cup of trahana (page 12)
⅛ teaspoon of cinnamon
Juice of 2 lemons
Salt and pepper to taste
2 tablespoons of chopped parsley

In a large saucepan, sauté the onion and celery in the oil until they are
soft. Add the tomatoes, broth, bay leaf, and basil. Bring to a boil and simmer
for 10 minutes. Add the trahana and cinnamon, and simmer for 20 minutes,
or until the soup thickens. Stir in the lemon juice; add salt and pepper and
continue to cook just until the soup again comes to a simmer. Sprinkle with
parsley and serve.

Fettuccelle and Yogurt Soup

SYRIA   Serves 4 to 6

5 cups of chicken broth
1 cup of fettuccelle (¼-inch-wide
    noodles), broken up
2 tablespoons of butter
1 medium-sized onion, finely
    chopped
Salt and pepper to taste

2 tablespoons of minced fresh mint
    leaves or 1 teaspoon of dried,
    crushed mint
2 tablespoons of minced fresh
    parsley
1½ cups of yogurt
2 egg yolks, beaten

In a saucepan, bring the chicken broth to a boil. Lower heat, and add the noodles. Cook noodles about 8 minutes or until they are *al dente*. Meanwhile, in a frypan over medium heat, melt the butter, add the onion, sprinkle with salt and pepper, and sauté until soft. Stir in the mint and parsley. Cook 1 minute and then stir it into the saucepan with the noodles. In a bowl stir the yogurt until smooth. Add the egg yolks and mix well. Stir about ½ cup of the hot soup, a spoonful at a time into the yogurt bowl. Pour this into the soup pot, stirring constantly. Taste for seasoning. Heat just to a simmer. Do not boil.

Stelline and Zucchini Soup

GREAT BRITAIN   Serves 6

2 tablespoons of butter
1 medium-sized white onion,
    chopped
Salt and pepper to taste
3 small zucchini (1 to 2 inches in
    diameter and 4 inches long),
    quarter lengthwise then cut into
    ¼-inch slices
6 cups chicken broth

½ cut of stelline ("star"-shaped pasta),
    cooked *al dente*, drained
1 egg
1 tablespoon of lemon
    juice   beaten
½ cup of freshly grated   together
    Double Gloucester
    cheese
2 tablespoons of minced parsley

In a large saucepan, over medium heat, heat the butter. Sauté the onion 5 minutes or until soft. Season with salt and pepper. Stir in the zucchini and chicken broth; bring to a boil, lower heat, and simmer, uncovered, for 3 minutes, or until the zucchini is barely tender. Add ½ cup of the soup liquid to the egg, lemon juice, and grated cheese mixture, and stir it and the pasta into the saucepan, mixing well. Taste for seasoning. Serve with parsley sprinkled on top of each serving.

IV

Fish and Shellfish

*A*MONG THE MOST VERSATILE and appealing pasta dishes are those made with fish or shellfish. In the latter category, one of the classic and most appreciated of seafood pasta dishes comes, not surprisingly, from the south of Italy, and was created by fishermen: pasta with clam sauce, both white and red. We prefer the white clam sauce, but the devotees of red claim that our favorite is vapid, theirs full of personality. Too full, we believe, the tomato masking the delicate flavor of the clams. Then, too, the red sauce devotees use *cheese* on their pasta. Unthinkable! Again, pasta people who know (or think they know) state that cheese also detracts from the flavor of clams, which should predominate. Backing our side on the cheese issue are the fishermen of Italy who first brought pasta and clams together. They wouldn't think of using cheese with it.

Then, there's another group who say that *both* Italian versions are pallid beside Chinese clams with black bean sauce. And there is an American school of thought that reasons that if clams and pasta are a good mating, then clams, oysters, and pasta is even better—and if oysters do not appeal, what about shrimp?

That is one of the pleasures of pasta, not only do its devotees disagree and go to some length to prove their point, but what finally emerges is that they all are right. Particularly when it comes to fish and shellfish. Pasta pairs with the produce of the sea in a phenomenal way. From France's pasta bows or butterflies with mussels, to Spain's sole with fettucce, to the Russian timballo of smoked salmon, the taste trail of seafood pasta is strewn with delights.

Linguine with Red Anchovy Sauce and Artichoke Hearts

SARDINIA   Serves 4 to 6

2 tablespoons of olive oil
2 two-ounce cans of flat fillets of anchovies (reserve the oil)
2 garlic cloves, minced
1 one-pound can of tomatoes, run through the food mill
½ teaspoon of salt

½ teaspoon of pepper
½ teaspoon of dry basil
4 canned artichoke hearts, coarsely chopped
1 pound of linguine, cooked *al dente*, drained
2 tablespoons of chopped parsley

In a saucepan, heat the olive oil and the oil from the 2 cans of anchovies. Reserve the anchovies for later. In the oil sauté the garlic until soft. Chop half of the anchovies and, along with the tomatoes, salt, pepper, and basil, add them to the saucepan. Bring the mixture to a boil, reduce to a simmer, and cook, uncovered, for 10 minutes. Stir occasionally. Add the artichoke hearts and cook for another 10 minutes. Toss half of the sauce with the linguine, serve the remainder on top. Garnish with the parsley and the remaining anchovy fillets.

Green Noodles and Anchovies

PORTUGAL   Serves 4

The Portuguese are justly proud of their anchovies, using them in just about everything except ice cream. Here is a pasta favorite rich with the little fishes.

½ cup of olive oil
6 Large garlic cloves, halved
2 two-ounce cans of anchovy fillets,
  · drained

4 tablespoons of butter, room
  temperature
1 teaspoon of black pepper
1 pound of green noodles, cooked
  al dente, drained

In a saucepan, heat the oil, and brown the garlic. Discard the garlic. Stir one-half of the anchovies into the saucepan, cooking, over low heat until they have disintegrated. Cut the remaining anchovies into ½-inch pieces and reserve. In a warm bowl, place the butter and pepper, add the pasta, and toss. Stir the cut-up anchovies into the hot oil-anchovy sauce. Add the hot garlicky oil-anchovy sauce a spoonful at a time (to prevent the pasta from becoming gummy), tossing each time, until all the sauce is used, and it is well blended with the pasta.

Spaghetti alla Chitarra with Anchovies

SICILY   Serves 4 to 6

3 tablespoons of olive oil
2 garlic cloves, minced
2 medium-sized white onions,
   chopped
8 medium-sized ripe tomatoes,
   peeled, seeded, and chopped
12 anchovy fillets, coarsely chopped

¼ cup of white raisins, chopped
¼ cup of pignoli (pine nuts)
1 tablespoon of minced fresh fennel
Salt and pepper to taste
1 pound of spaghetti alla chitarra
   ("guitar-string" spaghetti),
   cooked al dente, drained

In a saucepan, heat the oil, and sauté the garlic and onions until soft. Stir in the tomatoes, and cook over medium heat, stirring, for 10 minutes or until most of the water from the tomatoes has cooked off. Add the anchovies, raisins, pignoli, fennel, salt, and pepper. Simmer, stirring, for 3 minutes. Toss half of the sauce with the hot pasta, serve the remainder on top of the individual servings.

Noodles with Clams and Black Bean Sauce

CHINA   Serves 4 to 6

4 tablespoons of salted, fermented
   black beans, well rinsed
2 garlic cloves, minced
1 tablespoon of peanut oil
1 tablespoon of soy sauce ⎫
1 tablespoon of dry sherry ⎬ blended
1 teaspoon of sugar ⎭
2 cups of chicken broth

1 teaspoon of minced fresh ginger
4 tablespoons of chicken broth ⎫ blended
3 tablespoons of cornstarch ⎭
1 ten-ounce can of whole baby clams,
   drained (save broth for other
   uses)
1 pound of vermicelli, cooked al
   dente, drained

With a pestle and mortar (or a food processor) make a smooth paste of the black beans and garlic. In a wok or a deep saucepan, over medium heat, heat the peanut oil and stir-fry the beans-garlic mixture for 40 seconds. Blend the soy sauce, sherry, and sugar mixture into the bean mixture, and stir-fry for 40 seconds. Stir in the chicken broth and ginger. Bring to a boil. Blend in the chicken broth and cornstarch mixture, stirring until the liquid has thickened. Stir in the baby clams. Heat for 30 seconds. Spoon over the hot vermicelli, and toss well to blend.

Penne with White Clam Sauce

SICILY   Serves 6 to 8

These "pens" or "feather quills" are spectacular with this sauce. Since they are hollow, they collect the sauce and clams. This makes an excellent first course with roast poultry or meat to follow.

3 tablespoons of olive oil
3 garlic cloves, mashed
3 eight-ounce bottles of clam juice
1½ cups of dry white wine
3 eight-ounce cans of minced clams, strained (reserve the liquid)
2 garlic cloves, minced
Salt and black pepper to taste

½ teaspoon of red pepper flakes
5 tablespoons of butter, room temperature
1½ pounds of penne ("pens," short pasta tubes, cut diagonally at both ends), cooked *al dente*, drained
½ cup of chopped broadleaf parsley

In a deep saucepan, heat the oil and sauté the mashed garlic until brown. Discard the garlic. Remove the pan from the heat, as the next step would make oil splatter. When the oil has cooled a little, pour in the clam juice and the wine. Add the liquid from the canned clams and the minced garlic, salt, black pepper and red pepper. Cook, uncovered, over medium heat, until the sauce is reduced to slightly less than half. In a hot bowl, place the butter, add the cooked pasta, and toss well to blend. Stir the minced clams into the hot clam sauce. Spoon half of the sauce into the bowl of pasta, toss well. Add one-half of the parsley and toss well again to completely blend. Serve in hot dishes with the remaining clam sauce spooned on top of the individual servings and sprinkle with parsley.

Linque di Passeri Piccole with Crabmeat

SPAIN   Serves 4 to 6

The Spaniards, Portuguese, in fact all Europeans, use mainly Italian pastas, and like most of us everywhere, delight in the various imaginative sizes and shapes.

3 tablespoons of butter
2 tablespoons of olive oil
3 medium-sized white onions, chopped
3 celery ribs, scraped and chopped
2 garlic cloves, minced
3 tablespoons of minced broadleaf parsley
4 medium-sized, ripe fresh tomatoes, peeled, seeded, and chopped

1 teaspoon of salt
½ teaspoon of pepper
1½ teaspoons of paprika
1 pound of fresh or canned crabmeat, shell and cartilage removed, flaked
1 pound of lingue di passeri piccole (thin linguine), cooked al dente, drained

In a saucepan, heat the butter and oil, and sauté the onions, celery, and garlic until the onion is soft. Add the parsley, tomatoes, salt, pepper, and paprika, and cook over low heat for 25 minutes, stirring. Stir in the crabmeat and simmer for 5 minutes. Taste for seasoning. Toss the pasta with half of the sauce, and spoon the remaining sauce on top of the individual servings.

Lobster Tetrazzini

UNITED STATES   Serves 4

2 **two-pound lobsters,** boiled
   (reserve the water in which they
   are cooked), with meat removed
   and cut into strips or small,
   bite-sized pieces (save the coral)
5 **tablespoons of butter**
8 **medium-sized fresh mushrooms,**
   thinly sliced

3 **tablespoons of flour**
1 **cup of heavy cream**
2 **tablespoons of Madeira wine**
⅛ **teaspoon of mace**
   Salt and pepper to taste
½ **pound of vermicelli,** cooked *al
   dente*, drained

Reduce the liquid the lobsters were cooked in to 2 cups. In a saucepan, melt 3 tablespoons of butter and sauté the mushrooms for 5 minutes, or until tender-crisp. Remove the mushrooms with a slotted spoon and reserve. Add 2 tablespoons of butter to the saucepan, stir in the flour and the lobster coral, then gradually stir in the 2 cups of reduced cooking liquid, stirring until the sauce is smooth and thickened. Stir in the heavy cream and Madeira; add the mace, salt, and pepper to taste, and simmer, stirring, for 10 minutes. Stir in the lobster meat and the mushrooms; simmer just until heated through. Toss half of the lobster in its sauce with the pasta, serve the remainder on top of the individual servings.

Macarrones de Vigilia (Lenten Baked Macaroni)

SPAIN   Serves 4 to 6

24 mussels, at least, in their shells
2 medium-sized onions, chopped
1 garlic clove, chopped
3 tablespoons of butter
2 tablespoons of olive oil
4 large, ripe tomatoes, peeled and
   diced
1 cup of dry white wine

1½ pounds of sole, haddock, or any
   white fish, boned and cubed
Salt and pepper to taste
1 pound of ditalini (a small, short
   macaroni), cooked very *al dente*,
   drained
4 tablespoons of grated Romano
   cheese

Scrub the mussels and steam them until they open; strain the liquid through three layers of cheesecloth and discard the shells. Sauté the onions and garlic in 2 tablespoons of butter and the oil until the onions are soft. Add the tomatoes and wine and simmer for 15 minutes or until the sauce starts to thicken; add the fish cubes and the liquid from the mussels, the salt, and the pepper. Simmer 6 minutes or until the fish is still slightly undercooked. Stir in the mussels. In a buttered baking dish layer the pasta and the fish-mussel sauce. Sprinkle the cheese on top, dot with remaining butter and brown in a preheated 400-degree oven, about 20 minutes.

Farfalle with Mussels

FRANCE   Serves 4 to 6

3 dozen mussels, well scrubbed
3 shallots, minced
2 small white onions, minced
2 garlic cloves, mashed
3 tablespoons of chopped parsley
1 cup of dry white wine
6 peppercorns, crushed
2 tablespoons of butter

2 tablespoons of flour
½ cup of heavy cream
2 egg yolks
¾ pound of farfalle ("butterflies"), cooked *al dente*, drained
1 cup of grated Asiago or Parmesan cheese

In a large pot, place the mussels, shallots, onions, garlic, 1 tablespoon of parsley, wine, and the peppercorns. Cover, and cook over high heat for 5 minutes, or until the mussels open. Remove from the heat, drain, and shell the mussels, discarding the shells. Save all liquid in the pot. Keep mussels warm. Bring the pot of liquid to a boil, cook, uncovered, for 3 minutes. Strain through a fine sieve. In a saucepan, melt the butter, stir in the flour, and, over medium heat, cook, stirring until smooth and golden. Remove from heat, and gradually stir in the strained liquid. Place over low heat and cook, stirring, for 3 minutes, until the sauce is smooth. In a bowl, beat the egg yolks and cream together, and, off heat, stir it into the sauce. Place over low heat to warm, but do not boil or it will curdle. Add half of the mussels; toss the pasta with the sauce. Place the remaining mussels on top of the pasta. Sprinkle with remaining parsley. Serve the cheese on the side.

Rotelle with Mussels

PORTUGAL   Serves 4

2 quarts of well-scrubbed mussels
¼ cup of olive oil
3 tablespoons of chopped broadleaf
  parsley
3 garlic cloves, minced

4 medium-sized, ripe tomatoes,
  peeled, seeded, and coarsely
  chopped
Salt and pepper to taste
½ pound of rotelle (small pasta
  "wheels"), cooked *al dente*,
  drained

Place the mussels, evenly spaced in one layer in a large shallow pan; cover and cook in a preheated 300-degree oven for 5 minutes, or just until the mussels open. Watch carefully and from time to time shake the pan. Strain the liquid from the mussels through cheesecloth and reserve. Take the mussels from the shells, discarding the shells. In a deep saucepan, heat the oil, add the parsley and garlic, and cook for 3 minutes. Stir in the tomatoes, the strained mussel liquid, salt, and pepper. Simmer, uncovered, for 15 minutes. Add the mussels and cook for 5 minutes. Mix one-half of the sauce with the pasta and spoon the remainder over individual servings.

Noodle Fish Custard

JAPAN   Serves 4

2 cups of cooked udon (large soft
  noodles) or regular or egg
  noodles
2 tablespoons of soy sauce
4 eggs, beaten
4 cups of chicken broth

½ teaspoon of sugar
½ teaspoon of salt
1 cup of cubed cooked fish
5 whole scallions, chopped
8 medium-sized fresh mushrooms,
  thinly sliced

In a bowl place the noodles and 1 tablespoon of soy sauce, toss lightly and let the noodles set for 10 minutes to absorb the soy sauce. In another bowl, place the beaten eggs, broth, sugar, salt, and remaining soy sauce. Evenly divide the noodles and place them in 4 large custard cups or small casseroles; divide the fish, scallions, and mushrooms, and place on top of the noodles. Pour the egg-broth mixture over the contents of the cups. Set on a rack in a pan containing 1 inch of hot water (cups should be set above the water), cover, and steam for 20 minutes or until set.

Rice Noodles Kway Teow

MALAYSIA   Serves 6

Fresh rice noodles are available in Chinese shops.

4 tablespoons of peanut oil
4 small onions, thinly sliced
2 garlic cloves, minced
4 small fresh red chilies, seeded, chopped
¼ pound of lean pork, thinly sliced
½ pound of small squid, cleaned, thinly sliced

2 Chinese sausages, poached in hot water 5 minutes, drained, cut into thin diagonal slices
½ pound of shrimp, shelled, deveined
1 cup of fresh bean sprouts
2 pounds of fresh rice noodles
3 tablespoons of soy sauce
1 tablespoon of oyster sauce
2 large eggs, beaten
5 small scallions, chopped

In a wok or large frypan, heat 2 tablespoons of peanut oil over medium heat. Cook the onions, garlic, and chilies until soft. Stir in the pork, squid, and sausage, and cook, stirring for 5 minutes. Stir in the shrimp and bean sprouts, cook for 5 minutes, stirring. Remove from the heat. In another large frypan, heat the remaining oil until it smokes. Add the noodles, and stir-fry for 3 minutes. Stir in the soy and oyster sauces, tossing to mix well; then add

the beaten eggs, stirring over medium heat until the eggs are set. Add the
noodle mixture to the pork mixture, tossing well, but gently, to blend. Serve
on a hot platter with the scallions sprinkled on top.

Macaroni with Oysters and Clams

UNITED STATES   Serves 4

3 tablespoons of butter
2 small white onions, minced
1½ tablespoons of flour
1½ cups of light cream
1½ cup of grated Swiss cheese
1 teaspoon of lemon juice
½ teaspoon of salt
¼ teaspoon of paprika
⅛ teaspoon of cayenne pepper

1 teaspoon of Worcestershire sauce
½ pound of elbow macaroni, cooked
  very *al dente*, drained
2 cups of fresh or canned whole
  clams and oysters
⅓ cup of grated sharp ⎤
  Cheddar cheese ⎬ blended
⅓ cup of breadcrumbs ⎦

In a saucepan, heat the butter and sauté the onions until soft. Stir in the
flour, over low heat, blending it into a smooth paste. Slowly add the cream,
stirring into a smooth sauce, then blend in the cheese, lemon juice, salt, paprika, cayenne, and Worcestershire sauce. Taste for seasoning. In a casserole,
alternate layers of pasta, oysters, and clams. Pour the sauce over the layers
and sprinkle with the cheese and breadcrumbs mixture. Cook, uncovered, in
a preheated 350-degree oven for 35 minutes, or until bubbling and golden.

Mafalda with Oysters

UNITED STATES   Serves 4 to 6

We had this with some friends in Chincoteague, Virginia, a clamming and oystering center, home of the famed Chincoteague or salt oysters. Our hosts claimed that it had been served much this way in those parts for as long as anyone could remember, thus it probably originally came from England along with the early settlers.

4 tablespoons of butter
1 medium-sized white onion,
    minced
1 small red pepper, seeds and white
    ribs removed, minced
4 tablespoons of flour
2½ cups of light cream

1½ pints of fresh shelled oysters
⅓ teaspoon of cayenne
Salt and pepper to taste
1 pound of mafalda (broad, rippled
    noodles), cooked very *al dente*
¾ cup of buttered breadcrumbs

In a saucepan, melt the butter and cook the onion and pepper until soft. Stir in the flour, then gradually, over low heat, add the cream, cooking and stirring until the sauce is thick and smooth. Drain the oysters and stir the oyster liquor into the sauce; add the cayenne, and season with salt and peppers. In a buttered casserole, place half of the cooked noodles, cover with the oysters, spoon on 4 tablespoons of sauce, then cover with the remaining noodles. Spoon on the remaining sauce and evenly spread the breadcrumbs. In a preheated 350-degree oven, bake, uncovered, for 20 minutes, or until bubbling and browned.

Fettucce Riccie with Paprika-Fish

GREAT BRITAIN   Serves 6

3 tablespoons of butter
3 medium-sized white onions,
    chopped
1½ tablespoons of paprika
2 pounds of fillets of sole or any
    other white-fleshed fish, cut
    into bite-sized pieces.
1½ teaspoons of caraway seeds,
    crushed

1½ teaspoons of salt
½ teaspoon of pepper
1½ cups of boiling water
2 cups of sour cream, room
    temperature
1 pound of fettucce riccie
    (ripple-edged noodle), cooked
    al dente, drained
2 tablespoons of chopped fresh dill

In a large, deep saucepan, melt the butter and sauté the onions until soft. Stir in the paprika and cook 2 minutes. Add the fish, caraway seeds, salt, pepper, and water. Bring to a boil, lower to a simmer, cover, and cook for 3 minutes, or until the fish flakes easily with a fork. Drain the liquid from the fish. Carefully blend in the sour cream, pasta, and dill, and cook for 5 minutes or until heated through.

Pasta-and-Fish-Stuffed Peppers

DENMARK   Serves 6

3 medium-sized green ⎤ prepared for   1½ cups of cooked fish (cod, haddock,
   peppers   ⎟ stuffing by   etc.), diced
3 medium-sized red   ⎬ removing   2 cups of very *al dente*-cooked
   peppers   ⎟ seeds and   tubettini (a tiny, hollow pasta)
               ⎦ white ribs   drained
3 tablespoons of butter   1 teaspoon of salt
3 small white onions, chopped   ½ teaspoon of Tabasco sauce
2 small celery ribs (with leaves),   ¾ cup of breadcrumbs, blended with
   chopped   1 tablespoon of melted butter
2 tablespoons of flour
1 cup of tomato juice

Place the peppers in a pot of simmering salted water and cook until they can almost be pierced with a fork. They should not be tender, as they will be cooked some more. Drain the peppers. In a saucepan, melt the butter, and sauté the onions and celery until soft. Blend in the flour and the tomato juice, a little at a time, until the sauce is smooth and thickened. Mix in the fish, pasta, salt, and Tabasco sauce. Taste for seasoning. Stuff the peppers; top with the breadcrumbs, and in a baking dish, its bottom covered with hot water, bake, uncovered, in a preheated 375-degree oven for 20 minutes, or until the crumbs are brown.

Perciatelli with Sardines, Broccoli, and Eggplant

PORTUGAL   Serves 6 to 8

1 large bunch of broccoli
3 tablespoons of olive oil
1 large eggplant, peeled, diced
½ cup of beef broth
2 garlic cloves, minced
2 tablespoons of butter
1 teaspoon of salt
½ teaspoon of black pepper

¼ teaspoon of red pepper flakes
2 three-and-a-half-ounce cans of
    brisling sardines (double layer),
    drained
1 pound of perciatelli (a hollow string
    pasta, twice the thickness of
    spaghetti), cooked *al dente*,
    drained

Trim the broccoli and cook it in boiling, salted water until it is tender but still very crisp. Chop it coarsely. In a saucepan, heat the oil and sauté the eggplant for 5 minutes. Pour off the oil. Add the broccoli, the beef broth, garlic, butter, salt, black pepper, and red pepper, to the saucepan. Simmer the mixture for 5 minutes, stirring. Add the sardines and simmer for 3 minutes, or until the fish are hot and blended with the vegetables. Taste for seasoning. Gently toss half of the fish-vegetable sauce with the pasta and serve the remainder spooned on top of the individual servings.

Elbows Baked with Salmon

UNITED STATES

Serves 4

2 tablespoons of butter
2 tablespoons of flour
1½ cups of light cream
2 cups of grated Monterey Jack
   cheese
⅓ teaspoon of dry mustard
⅛ teaspoon of cayenne

½ teaspoon of salt
½ pound of small elbow macaroni,
   cooked very *al dente*, drained
1 small cucumber, thinly sliced
1 one-pound can of red salmon,
   drained and flaked
½ cup of buttered breadcrumbs

In a saucepan, melt the butter and stir in the flour, blending into a smooth paste. Gradually add the cream, stirring and simmering until the sauce is smooth and thickened. Blend in the cheese, mustard, cayenne, salt, pasta, cucumber, and salmon. Taste for seasoning. Pour into a buttered casserole, top with the breadcrumbs, and bake, uncovered, in a preheated 375-degree oven for 25 minutes, or until browned and bubbling.

Timballo of Trenette with Smoked Salmon

RUSSIA   Serves 6

We credit this to the Russians as it is said that it was a favorite of Tzar Nicholas II.

1 stick of butter
4 tablespoons of flour
2½ cups of milk
  A good pinch of nutmeg
2 ounces of cognac
  Salt and pepper to taste

12 ounces of trenette (narrow noodles), cooked very *al dente*, drained
6 ounces of thinly sliced smoked salmon, cut into narrow strips
⅔ cup of grated Gruyère cheese
⅔ cup grated Asiago or Parmesan cheese

In a saucepan, over low heat, melt 4 tablespoons of the butter. Stir in the flour and, stirring constantly, cook until you have a smooth paste. Add the milk a small amount at a time, and cook, stirring constantly, until you have a smooth sauce. Add the nutmeg and cognac, salt, and pepper. Set aside. Mix the cooked pasta with the remaining butter. Place one-third of the pasta in the bottom of a buttered baking dish. Arrange one-half of the salmon strips on it. Sprinkle with one-third of the cheeses. Spoon a light coating of the sauce over the cheeses. Arrange another layer of pasta, the remaining salmon, one-third of the cheese, and a few spoonfuls of sauce. Cover with the remaining pasta. Spoon on the sauce (the pasta should not be swimming in sauce but should be well covered with it). Sprinkle the remaining cheese on top, and bake in a preheated 350-degree oven for 20 minutes, or until top is golden. Let set a few minutes before serving.

Spaghettini with Scallops and Shrimp

SPAIN   Serves 6 to 8

2 cups of dry white wine
1 pound of shrimp, shelled, deveined
1 pound of bay scallops (use sea
    scallops, if necessary, but cut
    them into halves)
4 tablespoons of butter
4 shallots, finely chopped
12 medium-sized mushrooms, thinly
    sliced

2 tablespoons of minced broadleaf
    parsley
Salt and pepper to taste
2 tablespoons of flour
½ cup of heavy cream
1 pound of spaghettini, cooked *al
    dente*, drained
½ cup of grated Gruyère cheese

In a saucepan, bring the wine to a boil, add the shrimp, reduce to a simmer, cook for 3 minutes or until the shrimp are pink. Then remove the shrimp with a slotted spoon. Add the scallops to the wine, and cook until firm but not hard; remove with a slotted spoon. Strain the liquid. In a saucepan, melt the butter and sauté the shallots and mushrooms 5 minutes. Stir in the parsley, season with salt and pepper; stir in the flour and the strained liquid. Simmer, stirring, until the sauce thickens. Stir in the heavy cream, the scallops, and shrimp. Bring to a simmer to heat through, remove from the heat, and stir. Toss the scallops and shrimp in their sauce with the pasta; lightly sprinkle with cheese.

Green Lasagne with Shrimp

ITALY   Serves 4 to 6

Lasagne is one of the most famous and popular of the Italian pastas, so much so that it has almost become a cliché, too often served with a too heavy sauce, ground meat and cheese. Here is a welcome change of pace.

4 tablespoons of butter
2 medium-sized onions, finely chopped
3 tablespoons of flour
4 cups of light cream
  Salt and pepper to taste
1 teaspoon of curry powder
1 pound of green rippled lasagne, cooked very *al dente* in a large pot of salted water to which 2 tablespoons of olive oil have been added to keep the broad pasta from sticking; drain well (lay on damp towels to keep pasta from drying out)
2 pounds of shrimp, shelled, deveined and cooked 5 minutes, or until they begin to turn pink; cut each shrimp into halves
1 cup of grated Asiago or Parmesan cheese
  Paprika

In a saucepan, melt the butter and sauté the onions until soft. Blend in the flour and cook, stirring, until you have a thick paste. Gradually add the cream and cook, stirring, until you have a smooth, thickened sauce. Add salt, pepper, and curry powder. Blend well. Mask the bottom of a buttered baking dish with the sauce. Put in a layer of the lasagne, then a sprinkling of the shrimp. Spoon sauce over the shrimp. Continue layering until the shrimp and lasagne have all been used, saving enough sauce to coat the top well. Sprinkle with the cheese and a light dusting of paprika. Bake in a preheated 375-degree oven for 20 minutes or until the top is bubbling and golden.

Maruzze with Shrimp and Clams

UNITED STATES   Serves 4 to 6

Also called *conchiglie*, maruzze are large shells and make an impressive dish topped with this shellfish sauce prepared American style.

5 tablespoons of olive oil
4 garlic cloves, minced
2 seven-ounce cans of minced clams
    with their liquid
½ pound of shrimp, shelled,
    deveined, and coarsely chopped

Salt and pepper to taste
3 tablespoons of chopped parsley
1 pound of maruzze, cooked *al dente*,
    drained

In a saucepan, heat the oil and sauté the garlic until soft; be careful not to burn it. Add the clams and shrimp, and cook 3 minutes or just until the shrimp turn pink. Season with salt and pepper. Remove from the heat and stir in the parsley. Toss the pasta with half of the seafood sauce, top with the remainder. Americans serve a grated cheese with this, but it is better without. Cheese overwhelms the delicate flavor of the shellfish.

Basic Country-Style Noodles with Shrimp and Curry

JAPAN   Serves 4

Yes, the Japanese do use curry, and it is very popular there, in the rural areas as well as the cities. Here is a simple curry dish we had at an inn in the countryside.

2 tablespoons of peanut oil
1 large white onion, chopped
1 pound of fresh shrimp, shelled,
    deveined, and cut into
    medium-sized dices
4 cups of chicken broth
1 tablespoon of soy sauce
1 teaspoon of finely minced
    fresh ginger

2 tablespoons of Japanese curry
    powder
Salt to taste
2 tablespoons of cornstarch mixed
    with
3 tablespoons of water
4 cups of cooked soft udon noodles
    (or regular egg noodles)
4 scallions, chopped

In a saucepan, heat the oil and saute the onion for 4 minutes, or until soft. Add the shrimp and cook for 1 minute or until it turns pink (do not overcook as it will toughen). Stir in the broth, soy sauce, ginger, curry powder and salt. Bring to a simmer. Add the cornstarch paste and simmer, stirring, until thickened. Pour over the hot noodles and garnish with the scallions.

Garides Yahni (Braised Shrimp with Noodles)

GREECE   Serves 4 to 6

1 cup of chicken broth
1 cup clam broth
1½ pounds of uncooked shrimp in
    their shells
4 small onions, sliced
4 tablespoons of olive oil

1 two-pound can of Italian tomatoes,
    put through a food mill
1 tablespoon of chopped parsley
Salt and pepper to taste
1 pound of narrow egg noodles,
    cooked al dente, drained
2 tablespoons of butter

In a frypan, heat the chicken broth and clam broth to a boil. Add the shrimp, cover, and allow to come to a boil again. Remove from the fire, and, after 1 minute, remove the shrimp from the pan. Reserve 1 cup of the liquid.

When the shrimp are cool enough to handle, shell and devein them. Sauté the onions in the oil until soft. Stir in the tomatoes, parsley, salt, pepper and the liquid you reserved. Simmer for 20 minutes or until the sauce thickens and loses its watery consistency. Taste for seasoning. Add the shrimp, and simmer for 1 minute (do not overcook the shrimp; they should be pink and firm but not hard). Toss the hot noodles with the butter. Serve the sauce and shrimp spooned over the noodles.

Deep-Fried Shrimp-Stuffed Won Tons

CHINA   To make about 50

4 **tablespoons of peanut oil**
4 **scallions,** finely chopped (keep the green and white parts separate)
2 **pounds of shelled, deveined shrimp,** finely chopped
6 **water chestnuts,** drained, finely chopped
6 **dried black Chinese mushrooms,** soaked 35 minutes, drained, and finely chopped
1½ **tablespoons of sherry**

2 **tablespoons of soy sauce**
1½ **teaspoons of salt**
2 **teaspoons of cornstarch,** dissolved in 2 tablespoons of chicken broth
1 **recipe of won ton wrappers** (see page 14; or buy them ready-made in Oriental specialty shops)
3 **cups of vegetable oil,** for deep-frying

In a wok or frypan, heat the oil and stir-fry the white part of the chopped scallions for 1 minute; add the green part of the scallion and cook ½ minute. Add the shrimp, water chestnuts, mushrooms, sherry, soy sauce, and salt; stir-fry for 1 minute, or until the shrimp turn pink. Restir the cornstarch and the chicken broth mixture, stir it into the shrimp pan; cook, stirring until the mixture has thickened. Remove from the heat to cool to room temperature. Place a full teaspoon of the shrimp filling in the center of each square of won ton wrapper. Moisten a forefinger with water and run it around the edge of each won ton. Bring one corner up over the filling to the opposite corner, to form a triangle, and seal in the filling. Bring the corners of the long side of the triangle together, and seal the tips of them by pinching.

In a deep-fryer or wok, heat the oil to 375 degrees, or until a haze forms above it. Cook about 8 won tons at a time, for about 2 minutes, or until lightly browned and crisp. Drain on paper towels.

Fettucce with Sole

PORTUGAL   Serves 4

This is similar to the French classic, Sole Monte Carlo, but less complicated, and, for our taste, even better.

4 fillets of sole
Salt and pepper to taste
½ cup of dry white wine ⎫
¼ cup of clam juice   ⎪
1 cup of tomatoes, canned ⎬ blended
   or fresh, chopped,   ⎪
   drained   ⎪
2 tablespoons of minced ⎭
   broadleaf parsley

2 small white onions, chopped
½ pound of fettucce (broad noodles),
   cooked al dente, drained and
   tossed in 3 tablespoons of
   room-temperature butter and
   kept warm

Sprinkle the fillets with salt and pepper and roll, securing the rolls with toothpicks. Place the fillets in a deep saucepan; pour in the wine-clam juice-tomato-parsley blend and add the onions. Bring to a boil, reduce to a simmer, cover, and cook 5 minutes. Turn the fillets, cook 5 minutes. Remove the fish and set aside; keep warm. Over high heat, continue cooking the sauce for 2 minutes, stirring. Taste for seasoning. Spread the broad buttered noodles evenly on a hot serving platter; arrange the fillets on top. Spoon the hot sauce over them, and serve immediately.

Trenette in Tuna-Cream

SWITZERLAND   Serves 4 to 6

6 tablespoons of butter
1 pound of trenette (a narrow noodle), cooked *al dente*, drained
1 seven and a half-ounce can of tuna, drained, flaked

3 egg yolks, beaten with 1½ cups of heavy cream just until well blended
1½ cups of grated Swiss cheese
½ teaspoon of pepper
¼ teaspoon of nutmeg

In a deep saucepan, melt the butter and stir in the pasta, tuna, and egg yolks-and-cream mixture, cheese, pepper and nutmeg. Toss gently but well over low heat to completely blend and heat through. Taste for seasoning, adding salt, if necessary.

Tuna Kuroke

JAPAN   Serves 4

1 seven and a half-ounce can of tuna, drained, flaked
2 cups of cooked, soft, narrow noodles, drained
4 scallions (white part only), chopped

2 eggs, beaten
1 teaspoon of salt
Breadcrumbs for dredging
Oil for deep-frying
4 tablespoons of soy sauce

In a bowl, place the tuna, noodles, scallions, eggs, and salt. Blend and divide into 8 equal parts. Form patties, dredge with breadcrumbs and deep fry until evenly browned. Drain on paper towels and serve with the soy sauce.

Farfallette with Tuna and Yogurt Sauce

TURKEY   Serves 4

2 tablespoons of butter
2 tablespoons of olive oil
2 medium-sized onions, finely
    chopped
3 medium-sized, ripe tomatoes,
    peeled, seeded, and coarsely
    chopped

1 seven and a half-ounce can of tuna,
    drained, flaked
Salt and pepper to taste
½ pound of farfallette (small
    "butterflies"), cooked *al dente*,
    drained
½ cup of yogurt sauce

In a saucepan, heat the butter and the oil; sauté the onions until soft. Add the tomatoes, salt, and pepper, and simmer 15 minutes. Stir in the tuna and the hot pasta, mixing well. Top individual servings of pasta with 2 tablespoons of yogurt sauce.

YOGURT SAUCE

The Turks call this simple but tasty sauce "yogurt salcast."

½ **cup of plain yogurt**
 1 **garlic clove,** pushed through the
          garlic press
 ½ **teaspoon of salt**

In a bowl, combine all ingredients and beat well to blend thoroughly.

V

Poultry

*P*IGEON OR GAME HENS IN WALNUT SAUCE, "harissa" chicken, so hot it can start a grass fire, cubed duck with eggs, poached chicken wings, dilled chicken cutlets, chicken smothered in chickpeas. Interesting? Yes, but made doubly so with the innovative use of pasta. Pasta is even used to stuff a turkey and an Algerian steamed chicken. Read on and forever be a prisoner of pasta.

Algerian Steamed Pasta-Stuffed Chicken

Serves 4

2 cups of acini di pepe
   ("peppercorns"), cooked very *al*
   dente, drained
2 tablespoons of chopped walnuts
2 tablespoons of chopped toasted
   almonds
2 tablespoons of chopped white
   raisins
2 tablespoons of melted butter

⅛ teaspoon of ground cumin
⅛ teaspoon of ground cinnamon
⅛ teaspoon of ground ginger
1 tablespoon of honey
1 three and a half- or four-pound
   chicken
2 teaspoons of salt
2 tablespoons of butter
2 tablespoons of olive oil

In a large bowl, combine the acini di pepe, walnuts, almonds, raisins, melted butter, cumin, cinnamon, ginger, and honey, and blend well with a fork. Stuff the chicken with this mixture, close the cavity with skewers, and truss the chicken. Pour boiling water into a steamer to within 1 inch of the rack. Place the chicken on the rack, breast side up, bring water to a boil again. Cover the steamer and cook over medium heat for 40 minutes, or until the chicken is tender. Pierce a thigh, if the liquid runs pale yellow the bird is done, if slightly pink, it will need another few minutes. Pat the chicken dry with a dish towel or paper towels and sprinkle with the salt.

In a large saucepan, heat the butter and oil, and evenly brown the bird. Carve and spoon out the stuffing at the table.

Burmese Noodle Mix

Serves 6

1 pound of narrow egg noodles,
 cooked *al dente*, drained
½ cup of peanut oil
6 small onions, chopped
6 garlic cloves, chopped
4 chicken thighs, boned, thinly
 sliced
4 chicken livers, sliced
4 chicken gizzards, parboiled 10
 minutes, trimmed and sliced
2 tablespoons of soy sauce

¼ head of a small firm cabbage,
 shredded
3 celery ribs, scraped, shredded
6 dried black Chinese mushrooms,
 soaked in hot water 20 minutes,
 squeezed dry and sliced
6 scallions, thinly sliced
4 eggs, beaten
1 teaspoon of salt
½ teaspoon of pepper

Place cooked noodles on a flat dish; spoon 2 tablespoons of oil over them and toss. Set aside. In a wok or large frypan, heat 4 tablespoons of oil and cook the onions and garlic over medium heat until soft. Add the chicken thighs, livers, and gizzards, stir-fry 5 minutes. Stir in the soy sauce, cover and simmer for 10 minutes, or until the meat is tender. Add the vegetables, cook, stir-frying for 10 minutes. Vegetables should be tender but crunchy. In another frypan or small wok, place the noodles and cook for 2 minutes, tossing constantly to warm through. Place the noodles on a large hot serving dish, cover with the meats and vegetables. Meanwhile, add the remaining 2 table-spoons of oil to the pan in which you warmed the noodles and scramble the eggs; season them with salt and pepper. Serve the noodle dish garnished with the eggs.

Vermicelli with Chicken Cutlets

RUSSIA   Serves 6 to 8

There are many versions of this excellent dish. Some have breadcrumbs worked into the cutlets, some mix the chicken with game or with beef. We like this with a little pork mixed in.

1 stick (¼ pound) of butter, room
    temperature
3 large whole chicken breasts,
    skinned, boned, and ground
    (a food processor does the job
    in seconds)
½ pound of sausage meat
1½ teaspoons of salt
½ teaspoon of pepper
¼ teaspoon of mace
    Flour for dredging
    Breadcrumbs for dredging

1 egg, beaten with 1 tablespoon of
    water and 1 teaspoon of olive
    oil
6 tablespoons of butter
6 tablespoons of flour
2½ cups of chicken broth
1 cup of light cream
    Salt and pepper to taste
1½ teaspoons of dill weed
1 pound of vermicelli, cooked very
    al dente, drained

Place a large bowl in the freezer until it is very cold. Meanwhile, melt half of the stick of butter. Place the ground chicken, sausage meat, 1½ teaspoons of salt, ½ teaspoon of pepper, mace, and melted butter into the cold bowl. Mix well with your hands, then beat thoroughly with a spoon. Rechill in the freezer, but do not freeze. Place the flour and breadcrumbs for dredging on separate pieces of waxed paper. Place the egg mixture in a shallow dish. Form the chicken mixture into ½-inch-thick cutlets. Dredge them with flour, then dip in the egg mixture, then dredge with breadcrumbs. Chill again in the freezer for 6 minutes. In a large frypan, melt the remainder of the stick of butter (you may need more butter depending upon the number of cutlets), and brown the cutlets evenly. Set aside. In a saucepan, melt the 6 tablespoons of butter, add the flour, stirring it into a smooth paste. Gradually, over low heat, add the chicken broth and cream, and simmer until smooth and thickened, seasoning with salt and pepper. Stir in the dill weed. In a large cas-- serole, arrange the pasta, spoon one-third of the sauce over it, arrange the cutlets on top and cover with the remaining sauce. Place, uncovered, in a preheated 300-degree oven until bubbling.

Maruzzelle with Curried Chicken

INDIA   Serves 6

½ stick of butter
1 medium-sized onion, chopped
1 celery rib, scraped, finely chopped
1 small bay leaf
¼ teaspoon of dry mustard
1 tart apple, peeled, cored, and chopped
Salt and pepper to taste
3 tablespoons of flour
2 teaspoons (or more) of curry powder

1 cup drained, canned tomatoes, chopped
1 cup chicken broth
½ cup of coarsely ground cashews
1 tablespoon of currants
1½ cups of heavy cream
3 cups of cooked chicken, cut into ½-inch cubes
½ cup of chopped cooked ham
1 pound of maruzzelle (small shells), cooked al dente, drained

In a large saucepan, over medium heat, melt the butter. Add the onion, celery, bay leaf, mustard, apple, salt, and pepper. Stir and cook 7 minutes, or until the onion is soft. Stir in the flour and curry powder and cook 3 minutes, stirring constantly. Stir in the tomatoes and chicken broth. Cook 10 minutes, stirring frequently, until the sauce begins to thicken. Add the cashews, currants, and cream, simmer over low heat for 2 minutes. Stir in the chicken and ham and simmer for 1 minute. Taste for seasoning. Mix the cooked pasta shells with one-half of the chicken curry. Serve in hot rimmed soup bowls with the remaining sauce spooned on top.

Spaghetti Bucati with Chicken and Chick Peas

(Nohutlu Tavuk)

TURKEY   Serves 6

Called nohutlu tavuk, this unique dish is often made with pasta, sometimes with pilaf.

3 tablespoons of butter
12 small white onions (whole)
1 three and a half-pound chicken,
    cut into serving pieces
3 tablespoons of olive oil
4 medium-sized ripe fresh tomatoes,
    peeled, seeded, and coarsely
    chopped
1 cup of tomato juice

1 cup of chicken broth
2 one-pound four-ounce cans of
    chickpeas, drained
1½ teaspoons of salt
½ teaspoon of pepper
1 teaspoon of paprika
1 pound of spaghetti bucati (a thick
    hollow spaghetti), cooked *al
    dente*, drained

In a large saucepan, melt the butter and sauté the onions for 5 minutes.
Remove them with a slotted spoon and set aside. In the same saucepan
evenly brown the chicken. Set aside the chicken in its saucepan. In another
pan heat the olive oil, add the tomatoes and cook for 5 minutes; add the
tomato juice, and chicken broth, cover the pan, and simmer for 20 minutes.
Add the chickpeas, reserved onions, salt, pepper, and paprika. Simmer,
covered, for 10 minutes. Pour this mixture over the chicken in its pan; cover
and simmer for 25 minutes, or until the chicken is fork-tender. Taste for
seasoning. Toss half of the sauce with the cooked hot pasta, serve the remainder on top of individual servings with the chicken on the side.

Fettucce Riccie with Chicken

FRANCE   Serves 6

2 three-pound broiler chickens, cut
   into serving pieces
Flour for dredging
1 stick (¼ pound) of butter
2 white onions, finely chopped
2 garlic cloves, minced
¼ teaspoon of marjoram
7 tablespoons of flour
4 cups of chicken broth

1 one-pound can of tomatoes,
   drained, chopped
1 teaspoon of salt
½ teaspoon of pepper
12 very small white onions, whole
¾ cup of dry white wine
1 pound of fettucce riccie (a narrow,
   rippled noodle), cooked *al dente*,
   drained

Dredge the chicken pieces with flour; shake off the excess. In a saucepan, melt the butter, and over medium heat, brown the chicken evenly. Remove the chicken and set aside. To the same pan, add the chopped onions, garlic, and marjoram, cooking until the onion is soft. Stir in the 7 tablespoons of flour, then gradually blend in the chicken broth, stirring until the sauce is smooth and thickened. Add the browned chicken to the sauce, also the tomatoes, salt, pepper, whole onions, and wine; stirring well. Bring to a boil, then simmer, covered for about 20 minutes, or until the chicken is fork-tender. Taste for seasoning. Place the hot cooked noodles on a hot serving plate, arrange the chicken on top and cover with the sauce.

Tagliatelle with Chicken and Spinach

ITALY   Serves 4

1 ten-ounce package of fresh spinach
Salt and pepper to taste
Pinch of nutmeg
5 tablespoons of butter
2 tablespoons of flour
1½ cups of chicken broth
1 cup of medium cream
¾ cup of grated Asiago or Parmesan cheese

2 cups of bite-sized pieces of cooked chicken, preferably moist breast
7 rounds (or ½ pound) of tagliatelle (narrow noodles, sometimes "nest"-shaped), cooked very al dente, drained
2 tablespoons of breadcrumbs

Fill a 4-quart pot three-quarters full of water. Bring to a boil, stir in the fresh spinach, let the water come to a boil again, and, with a large fork, remove the spinach; drain it well. Coarsely chop the spinach and season with salt, pepper, nutmeg, and 2 tablespoons of the butter. Set it aside. In a saucepan, melt the remaining butter, stir in the flour, and, stirring constantly, cook until the paste is thick and smooth. Gradually add the chicken broth and cream, stirring until the sauce is medium-thick. Season to taste. Stir in one-half of the cheese. In a bowl, combine the chicken and pasta. Mix with one-fourth of the sauce. In a deep baking dish, arrange the spinach in a thick layer. Spoon one-fourth of the sauce over it. Spread the pasta-chicken mixture over the spinach. Cover with the remaining sauce. Sprinkle with breadcrumbs and remaining cheese. Cook in a preheated 375-degree oven for half an hour, or until the sauce bubbles and the top is golden.

Cavatelli with Chicken and Sausage

ITALY   Serves 6

2 one-pound, twelve-ounce cans of
   Italian plum tomatoes, put
   through the food mill
1 teaspoon of salt
½ teaspoon of pepper
6 sweet Italian fennel sausages
   (finocchiona)
2 tablespoons of olive oil
1 three and a half-pound chicken,
   cut into serving pieces
Salt and pepper to taste

3 medium-sized white onions,
   chopped
6 medium-sized mushrooms, sliced
1 large red pepper, seeds and white
   ribs removed, coarsely
   chopped
2 garlic cloves, minced
1½ teaspoons of oregano
½ cup of chicken broth
½ cup of dry red wine
1 pound of cavatelli (a short, curled
   pasta), cooked *al dente*, drained

Place the tomatoes, salt, and pepper in a deep saucepan, and cook, un-covered, stirring from time to time, for 20 minutes, or until most of the water has evaporated. In another saucepan, place the sausages, cover with boiling water and simmer for 10 minutes. Prick the sausages in several places and drain. In a large, deep frypan, heat the oil and brown the sausages evenly. Remove and cut them into medium-thick slices; set aside. Add the chicken to the same frypan from which the sausages have been removed, season with salt and pepper, and brown evenly. Return the sausage slices to the frypan with the chicken. Add the onions, mushrooms, red pepper, garlic and oregano. Pour in the cooked tomatoes, the chicken broth, and wine; stir well. Cover and simmer for 20 minutes, or until the chicken is fork-tender. Taste for seasoning. Remove the chicken pieces. Toss the hot pasta with half of the sausage-tomato-vegetable sauce. Spoon the remainder of the sauce on top of the individual servings with the chicken on the side.

Fedelini with Fowl

SWITZERLAND

Serves 6 to 8

5 slices of bacon, diced
4 tablespoons of butter
2 three and a half-pound chickens, cut into serving pieces
3 medium-sized white onions, chopped
3 garlic cloves, minced
8 large, ripe tomatoes, peeled, seeded, and chopped
1 cup of red wine
½ teaspoon of oregano
Pinch of dry rosemary
Salt and pepper to taste

12 medium-sized fresh mushrooms, cut into thick slices, cooked in 2 tablespoons of butter and 1 tablespoon of lemon juice for 2 minutes
2 cups of shelled small fresh peas, cooked until just tender in a small amount of salted water with 1 teaspoon of sugar, and drained
1 pound of fedelini (one of the thinnest of spaghettis), cooked *al dente*, drained

In a large pot, cook the bacon for 7 minutes; add the butter. When the butter has melted, brown the chicken pieces evenly, a few at a time. Remove the chicken and set it aside. Add the onions and garlic to the pot, cooking until the onions are soft. Replace the chicken; add the tomatoes, wine, oregano, rosemary, salt, and pepper. Stir; bring to a boil; reduce the heat to a simmer, cover, and cook 25 minutes, or until the chicken is fork-tender. In a large hot bowl, combine the hot mushrooms, hot peas, and hot pasta, and blend well. The Swiss arrange the pasta on a large hot serving platter surrounded by the chicken and covered with sauce.

German Ravioli

Serves 4 to 6

1 recipe of spaetzle (page 11)
2 tablespoons of butter
1 medium-sized onion, minced
1 pound of uncooked chicken, veal,
   or lean pork, ground
2 slices of dry white bread soaked in
   milk

1 ten-ounce package of fresh spinach
   (or 1 ten-ounce package of
   frozen, cooked according to
   package directions) cooked,
   cooled, squeezed dry, and finely
   chopped
1 large egg, beaten
   Salt and pepper to taste
¼ teaspoon of nutmeg

Make the spaetzle dough and let it stand, covered with a damp cloth, while you prepare the filling. Melt the butter in a frypan, add the onion, and cook until onion is soft. Stir in the chicken, veal, or pork and cook 15 minutes, or until it darkens. Remove from the heat. Squeeze the milk from the bread; stir the bread and the spinach into the frypan. Stir in the egg, salt, pepper, and nutmeg; blend well. Divide dough into three parts and on a lightly floured board, roll each as thin as possible. Cut it into 4-inch squares. Place a generous tablespoon of the filling just off center on each square. Moisten edges with water, fold over into a triangle, and seal. In a large pot of mildly boiling salted water, cook 3 or 4 of the stuffed pastas at a time, for 10 minutes, or until they rise to the surface. Drain. Serve in beef or chicken broth, or with tomato sauce spooned on top.

Another tasty sauce to serve with German Ravioli is German onion sauce (page 212).

Mostaccioli with "Harissa" Chicken

LIBYA   Serves 6

⅓ cup of olive oil
3 medium-sized white onions,
   chopped
3 celery ribs, scraped, chopped
12 chicken thighs
½ teaspoon of cayenne
   Salt and pepper to taste
10 medium-sized fresh ripe tomatoes,
   peeled, seeded, and chopped
3 tablespoons of lemon juice
1 cup of small fresh green beans
1 cup of small fresh shelled peas

1 cup of fresh shelled baby limas
1 pound of mostaccioli (little
   "moustaches," medium-sized
   pasta tubes), cooked al dente,
   drained
½ cup of fresh coriander leaves,
   chopped
1 teaspoon of harissa (a very, very
   hot North African red pepper
   condiment) or 1 teaspoon of red
   pepper flakes and a dash of
   tabasco sauce

In a large deep pot, heat the oil and sauté the onions and celery until soft. Push vegetables aside and brown the chicken thighs evenly, seasoning with cayenne, salt, and pepper. Add the tomatoes, lemon juice, beans, peas, and limas. Cover and cook in a preheated 325-degree oven for 40 minutes, or until the chicken and vegetables are fork-tender. Stir in the pasta tubes, coriander, and hot pepper; bring to a simmer, stir well, and serve.

New Delhi Spaghettini with Chicken

INDIA   Serves 6

In India, most of the noodle or pasta dishes are sweet, and served as dessert. But this delicious exception is popular in Delhi where we have eaten it in several variations.

3 whole chicken breasts, boned,
skinned, and cut into 1-inch
cubes
½ teaspoon of cayenne pepper
½ teaspoon of black pepper
2 teaspoons of salt
2 tablespoons of cornstarch
1 egg white
⅓ cup of peanut oil

4 small onions, chopped
4 garlic cloves, minced
4 fresh chilies, seeded, chopped
6 fresh mushrooms, thinly sliced
1 tablespoon of vinegar
1 teaspoon of sugar
1 pound of spaghettini, cooked *al
dente*, drained

In a bowl, place the chicken, cayenne, black pepper, 1 teaspoon of salt, cornstarch, and egg white. Blend well. In a frypan, heat the oil over medium heat and brown the chicken evenly. With a slotted spoon, remove the chicken, leaving about 2 tablespoons of oil, and all of the browned particles. Add the onions, garlic, and chilies, and cook for 5 minutes, stirring. Stir in the mushrooms, the remaining salt, the vinegar, and the sugar, and cook stirring for 4 minutes. Add the cooked chicken, blending it with the vegetables, and cook for 2 minutes. Taste for seasoning. Place the hot spaghettini on a hot platter and spoon the sauce over it. Toss with two forks, then serve.

Noodle Chicken Kama Meshi

JAPAN   Serves 4

12 chicken wings
2 tablespoons of peanut oil
1 cup of shredded carrots (scrape
before shredding)
1 cup of minced whole scallions

4 cups of cooked udon noodles (or
regular egg noodles), cooked
soft, drained
1 teaspoon of salt
½ teaspoon of pepper
½ cup of small sweet peas, cooked

Cut off the tips from the chicken wings, and place both wings and tips in a pot; barely cover with hot water and simmer until tender. In a saucepan, heat the oil and sauté the carrots and scallions for 2 minutes. Do not overcook, as they should be crunchy. Blend in the noodles, salt, pepper, and peas. Add 4 tablespoons of the broth from the chicken pot, toss, and serve with the tender chicken wings (discard the tips) on top.

Chicken and Fried Noodles

CHINA   Serves 6

1 pound of very fine noodles, cooked (about half done) very *al dente*, drained, spread out evenly on a plate and refrigerated for 2½ hours

⅓ cup of peanut oil

2 whole, uncooked chicken breasts, boned, and cut into thin strips

3 tablespoons of cornstarch

8 small fresh mushrooms, thinly sliced

1 cup of canned, drained bean sprouts

2 tablespoons of soy sauce

2 cups of chicken broth

Salt to taste

3 scallions, finely chopped

In a saucepan, heat 2 tablespoons of the oil, stir in the chicken and cook for 6 minutes, browning slightly. Sprinkle with the cornstarch, stir in the mushrooms and cook, stirring, for about 10 minutes, or until the liquid from the mushrooms thickens. Stir in the bean sprouts, soy sauce, and chicken broth; bring to a boil, stirring. Reduce to a simmer and cook for 8 minutes, or until the chicken is tender. Taste for seasoning; add salt if necessary. In a frypan, heat the remaining oil. Place the noodles in the hot oil, pressing down with a spatula to form a pancake. Cook over medium heat for 5 minutes, or until the noodles are brown and heated through; turn and brown the other side. Center the noodle-cake on a hot serving platter; cover with the chicken in its sauce; sprinkle with the chopped scallions.

Chicken and Noodles Burmese Style

Serves 6

2 cups of fresh or dried, grated
   coconut
3 cups of milk
⅓ cup of peanut oil
2 medium-sized white onions,
   chopped
4 garlic cloves, minced
1 teaspoon of powdered ginger
1 tablespoon of curry powder
2 whole chicken breasts, boned, cut
   into small cubes

6 chicken thighs, boned, cut into
   small cubes
1 cup of boiling water
1½ teaspoons of salt
⅓ cup of cornstarch ⎫
⅓ cup of cold water ⎭ blended
1 pound of very broad egg noodles,
   cooked *al dente*, drained
½ teaspoon of dried ground chili
   peppers
6 small scallions, finely chopped
4 hard-cooked eggs, chopped

Place the coconut and milk in a deep saucepan; bring to a boil, remove from the heat, and let stand for 35 minutes. Squeeze the liquid from the coconut back into the milk, then discard the coconut. In another saucepan, heat the oil and stir in the onions, garlic, ginger, and curry powder. Blend well and cook over medium heat for 10 minutes. Stir in the chicken, and cook, stirring frequently, for 15 minutes. Pour in 2 cups of the coconut milk, the boiling water and the salt. Blend well, cover, and simmer for 25 minutes, or until the chicken is fork-tender. Mix in the blended cornstarch and water, bring to a boil, and stir. Lower the heat and simmer for 10 minutes. Stir in the rest of the coconut milk; simmer 5 minutes. Place the cooked noodles on a large hot serving dish; spoon on the chicken in its sauce, then sprinkle on the peppers, scallions, and eggs.

Penne Rigati with Chicken

SWITZERLAND   Serves 6

6 medium-sized ripe tomatoes,
    peeled, seeded, and chopped
2 medium-sized white onions,
    chopped
½ cup of chicken broth
1 tablespoon of olive oil
6 slices of bacon, julienne style
1 whole chicken breast, skin and
    bones removed, julienne style
2 tablespoons of flour

1½ teaspoons of salt
½ teaspoon of pepper
¾ cup of dry white wine
2 garlic cloves, minced ⎫ blended into
4 basil leaves, minced   ⎬   a paste
4 tablespoons of butter ⎭
1 pound of penne rigati (grooved,
    hollow tubes), cooked *al dente*,
    drained
1 cup of grated Gruyère cheese

In a saucepan, place the tomatoes, the onions, and the chicken broth; cook 10 minutes. In another saucepan, heat the oil and brown the bacon and chicken. Sprinkle flour, salt, and pepper over the bacon and chicken; pour in the wine, and simmer until half of it has evaporated. Stir in the tomato mixture; bring to a boil, then simmer, uncovered for 20 minutes. Stir the garlic-basil-butter paste into the tomato mixture; cook 5 minutes. Taste for seasoning. Mix the cooked pasta with half of the sauce; serve the remaining sauce and cheese on top of the individual servings.

Pigeon (or Chicken or Duck) and Tagliolini

TUNISIA   Serves 4 to 6

2 pigeons (or 1 duck, or 1 chicken),   3 cardamon pods, cracked
   poached until tender, cooled,   1 teaspoon of salt
   boned; save stock   ½ teaspoon of pepper
12 ounces of tagliolini (or a noodle of   1 tablespoon of olive oil
   your choice)   2 tablespoons of chopped parsley
4 eggs

Cut the boned fowl into small cubes. Bring the stock in which the fowl
was poached to a boil, and cook the noodles very *al dente*. Remove the pasta
with pasta tongs, shaking off excess stock but leaving the noodles with a film
of the poaching stock. In a bowl, beat the eggs, add the pigeon (or duck
or chicken) cubes, noodles, cardamom pods, salt, and pepper. Blend well.
In a large frypan, heat the oil; pour in the egg-fowl cubes-noodles mixture
and cook over low heat for 30 minutes, or until completely set. Place under a
broiler until golden brown and serve sprinkled with parsley.

Vermicelli with Pigeons (or Cornish Game Hens) and Walnut Sauce

TURKEY   Serves 4 to 6

3 pigeons (or game hens)
1 quart of water
1 quart of chicken broth
2 medium-sized onions, quartered
2 medium-sized carrots, quartered
2 celery ribs, quartered
1 teaspoon of salt
½ teaspoon of pepper

4 slices of white bread,
   without crusts
2 cups of shelled walnuts
2 garlic cloves, crushed
2 tablespoons of olive oil
1 teaspoon of paprika
1 pound of vermicelli, cooked *al
   dente*, drained

Place the birds in a large pot; add the water, broth, onions, carrots, celery, salt, and pepper. Bring to a boil, cover, and simmer for 1½ hours, or until the birds are fork-tender. Remove from the stock, cool, remove skin and bones, and cut the birds into 2-inch pieces. Strain and save the stock. In a cup of the stock, soak the bread then squeeze it dry. Place the bread, walnuts, and garlic in a blender or food processor and blend into a paste. Blend in 1 cup of the cooking stock gradually. Then, in small amounts, blend in more stock until you have a medium sauce (it should not be thick). Taste for seasoning.

In a saucepan, over low heat, heat the oil and paprika until the oil is red. Mix the cut-up fowl with one-third of the walnut sauce and toss with the hot pasta. On a hot serving platter, arrange the pasta, spoon the remaining walnut sauce over it, then over that, carefully pour the hot paprika-oil, leaving most of the paprika in the pan.

Pasta-Stuffed Turkey

ITALY   Serves 6 to 8

2 tablespoons of olive oil
6 sweet Italian sausages
2 celery ribs, scraped and chopped
2 medium-sized white onions,
    chopped
1 ten-ounce package of spinach
    (uncooked), chopped
2 eggs, beaten
¼ teaspoon of leaf sage
⅛ teaspoon of mace
½ teaspoon of oregano

½ teaspoon of thyme
1½ teaspoons of salt
½ teaspoon of pepper
⅓ cup of grated Asiago or Parmesan
    cheese
½ pound of tubettini (tiny, hollow
    soup pasta), cooked very *al
    dente*, drained
1 ten-pound turkey
5 tablespoons of soft butter
Salt to sprinkle on outside of bird

Remove the skin from the Italian sausages. In a deep saucepan, heat the oil and cook the sausage meat for 10 minutes, breaking it up. Stir in the celery and onions and cook 3 minutes. Add the chopped spinach, eggs, sage, mace, oregano, thyme, salt, pepper, and cheese. Stir in the cooked pasta, blending well. Do not stuff the bird until the stuffing has cooled. Stuff and truss the bird. Rub it well with the soft butter, and sprinkle with salt. Place the turkey on its side on a rack in a roasting pan. Cook, uncovered, in a preheated 425-degree oven for 15 minutes. Turn the bird onto its other side; baste well, and cook for another 15 minutes. Baste; cover with aluminum foil and turn breast up. Lower the oven heat to 375 degrees and cook the turkey 20 minutes per pound, counting the half hour the bird has already cooked. Baste from time to time. Prick a thigh for doneness; if juice runs clear it is cooked, if it is pink-tinged cook another 10 minutes and test again.

HOSTOVIEH

VI

Meats

*P*ASTA WITH MEAT is a double blessing, for the sauce that will crown the pasta has itself been cooked with the meat. Sometimes the meat is served as a separate course, sometimes with the pasta. But however the meat is served, it has imparted its powerful personality to the sauce, and, paired with the pasta, the result is remarkable.

Strong praise? Strong recipes back up our pronouncement: Jim Anelli's pot roast sauce with butterflies; a Greek leg of lamb sauce with orzo; veal baked with pasta Turkish style; a matchless French melding of mushrooms, sausage, and pasta; an Austrian goulash with noodles; Chinese soft fried noodles with pork.

Austrian Ham-Noodle Cake

Serves 6

10 tablespoons of sweet butter
4 scallions, white part only, finely
  chopped
1 pound of very broad noodles,
  cooked very *al dente*, drained,
  and cut into 1-inch pieces

1 cup of sour cream
5 eggs, beaten
2 cups of diced cooked ham
½ teaspoon of salt
1 teaspoon of pepper
1 cup of breadcrumbs

In a large frypan, melt half of the butter and cook the scallions for 3 minutes, or until soft. Add the noodles and the remaining butter and blend until the noodles are evenly coated. Remove from the heat. In a bowl blend the sour cream, eggs, ham, salt, and pepper. Mix with the scallion-noodle mixture. Taste for seasoning. Generously butter a large casserole and spread the breadcrumbs in an even layer. Spoon in the ham-noodle-cream mixture. Bake, uncovered, in a preheated 350-degree oven for 50 minutes or until set. Loosen the edges of the casserole with a knife, and invert on a serving plate. The ham-noodle cake is served unmolded bottom side up.

Authentic Goulash and Noodles

AUSTRIA

Serves 6

4 small white onions, sliced
6 tablespoons of butter
1 pound of veal shoulder, cut into
  1-inch cubes
1 pound of pork loin, cut into cubes
  slightly smaller than the veal
  cubes

2 tablespoons of flour
Salt and pepper to taste
1 teaspoon of paprika
4 cups of beef broth
1 pound of noodles, cooked
  al dente, drained

In a heavy casserole sauté the onions in 4 tablespoons of butter until soft; add the veal and pork cubes and simmer for 15 minutes, stirring once or twice. Sprinkle with the flour and blend in the salt, pepper, paprika, and beef broth. Stir well. Simmer for 1 hour, covered, or until the meat is tender and the liquid thickened, stirring often. If the meat should become tender before the sauce thickens, remove the cover. Toss the noodles in the remaining butter. Serve the goulash tossed with the buttered noodles.

Spaghettini Alla Trastevere

ITALY   Serves 4 to 6

This dish is unique to that part of Rome which lies across the Tiber, the so-called Trastevere district.

3 tablespoons of butter
½ pound of lean bacon, diced
1 tablespoon of coarsely milled black
   pepper

1 pound of spaghettini, cooked
   al dente, drained
½ cup of grated Romano cheese

In a saucepan, melt the butter and cook the bacon until crisp. Stir in the pepper, blending well. Toss half of the bacon mixture with the cooked, hot pasta, serve the remaining bacon on top. Sprinkle with the cheese. If black pepper isn't your thing, reduce it according to taste. But the classic dish is very peppery.

Penne with Bacon and Ham

UNITED STATES   Serves 4 to 6

This is an American adaptation of Carbonara, an Italian classic. The cheese, ham, and egg yolks should be at room temperature.

¼ **pound of lean bacon,** cut into 1-inch pieces

3 **medium-sized white onions,** chopped

1 **pound of penne** (short pasta tubes, cut diagonally on each end), cooked *al dente*, drained

2 **tablespoons of broad leaf parsley,** chopped

1 **cup of Fontina cheese,** finely diced

⅔ **cup of finely shredded ham,** preferably prosciutto

2 **egg yolks,** beaten

½ **teaspoon of hot red-pepper flakes**

1 **teaspoon of black pepper**

1 **cup of grated Romano cheese**

In a frypan, cook the bacon until crisp; remove and drain on paper towels. Cook the onions in the bacon fat until soft. In a hot bowl, place the hot cooked pasta. Add the bacon, onion, parsley, Fontina cheese, ham, egg yolks, red-pepper flakes, black pepper, and half of the grated cheese. Toss well with two wooden forks. Pass the remainder of the cheese at the table.

Beef and Macaroni Mix-Up

EAST AFRICA   Serves 6

2 **pounds of round steak,** cut into 1-inch cubes

2 **teaspoons of salt**

1 **teaspoon of pepper**

1 **cup of grated, sharp, aged Cheddar cheese**

1½ **cups of breadcrumbs**

2 **eggs,** beaten

Vegetable oil for deep-frying

1 **pound of elbow macaroni,** cooked very *al dente*, drained

1 **cup of sour cream**

Sprinkle the meat cubes with 1 teaspoon of salt and ½ teaspoon of pepper. Dredge the meat cubes with half of the grated cheese, then with the breadcrumbs. Dip them into the beaten egg, then dredge again with the breadcrumbs. In a fryer or deep saucepan, heat the oil to a sizzling 375 degrees. (Use enough oil so that the meat cubes will be completely immersed in hot oil when frying.) Fry a few pieces of meat at a time, for about 1 minute each, or until golden. Drain the meat on paper towel. In a buttered casserole, layer the cooked macaroni, sprinkling it with the remaining salt, pepper, and cheese. Mask the layer with the sour cream. Arrange the steak cubes on top. Bake, uncovered, in a 400-degree oven for 15 minutes or until the sour cream starts to bubble.

Rigatoni with Fast Bolognese Sauce

ITALY   Serves 4 to 6

Bolognese sauce is probably the most famous of all pasta sauces, and has several variations, most of which contain at least twenty ingredients and most of which are time-consuming. This one isn't. It utilizes Filetto Sauce, which can be prepared ahead in large batches and frozen, thereby reducing at least two cooking steps.

2 tablespoons of olive oil
2 garlic cloves, minced
1½ pounds of ground top sirloin
   Salt and pepper to taste
4 cups of Filetto Sauce (page 206)
6 medium-sized fresh mushrooms,
      thinly sliced, sautéed in butter
      2 minutes

8 large chicken livers, trimmed,
      coarsely chopped
½ cup of heavy cream
1 pound of rigatoni (large grooved
      pasta tubes), cooked *al dente*,
      drained
1 cup of grated Asiago or Parmesan
      cheese

In a pot, heat the oil and sauté the garlic until soft. Stir in the ground meat, season with salt and pepper, cook 6 minutes over medium heat, breaking the meat as it cooks. The meat should be pink. To the pot containing the ground meat add the Filetto Sauce, the mushrooms, and the chicken livers; simmer for 5 minutes, or until the livers are cooked but pink inside. Stir in the heavy cream. When the sauce is hot, toss half of it with the hot cooked pasta; add ½ cup of cheese, toss again. Serve the remaining sauce spooned on top of the individual servings. Sprinkle each with the rest of the cheese. Sit back and listen to the cheers.

Caribbean Spaghetti with Chorizo Sausages

Serves 6 to 8

2 tablespoons of lard
2 ounces of salt pork, chopped
4 ounces of cured ham, chopped
2 medium-sized white onions, chopped
2 small ripe tomatoes, skinned, seeded, and chopped
1 small green pepper, cored, seeded, and chopped
2 sweet chili peppers, seeded, chopped
10 green olives, pitted, chopped

2 teaspoons of capers, rinsed and drained
6 chorizo sausages, poached, skinned, and thinly sliced
2 four-ounce cans of tomato sauce
¼ cup of achiote lard
1 pound of spaghetti, cooked very *al dente*, drained
Salt and pepper to taste
¾ cup of grated Asiago or Parmesan cheese

In a large pot, melt the lard and brown the pork and ham. Stir in the onions, cook for 5 minutes. Add the tomatoes, peppers, olives, capers, and sausages. Cook 10 minutes. Stir in the tomato sauce, the achiote lard, and the cooked spaghetti. Cover the pot and cook over medium heat for 10 minutes. Taste for seasoning, adding salt and pepper, if necessary. Serve sprinkled with grated cheese.

Stuffed Dumplings (Kreplachs)

JEWISH   Makes about 40

DOUGH

2 **cups of flour**
2 **eggs**

4 **tablespoons of cold water**
1 **teaspoon of salt**

In a large bowl, place the flour, form a well in the center, place the eggs in the well with 2 tablespoons of water and the salt. Stir the flour into the eggs and water; stirring until the dough can be formed into a ball. Add the remaining water, if necessary. On a lightly floured pastry board, place the ball of dough and knead it well with your hands. When it is smooth and malleable, wrap it and let it set for 40 minutes.

STUFFING

4 **tablespoons of butter**
3 **medium-sized white onions,** finely chopped

¾ **pound of finely ground top sirloin**
1 **egg,** beaten
Salt to taste

In a frypan, melt the butter and cook the onions until they are soft; add the beef, and stir, cooking for 8 minutes. Stir in the egg and salt, blending well. Cool for 40 minutes.

On a lightly floured pastry board, roll out the dough with a rolling pin until it is about ⅛ inch thick. With a pastry wheel, cut the dough into 2-inch squares. Place a teaspoon of stuffing in the center of each square, rub the outside edge of dough with cold water. Fold the square of dough into a triangle, encasing the stuffing; firmly press the edges closed with your fingers. In a large pot, place three quarts of warm water; bring to a boil, then reduce to a simmer. With a slotted spoon, lower the dumplings into the simmering water a few at a time and cook for 20 minutes. Use these in soup, or crisp them under the broiler and serve with roast chicken. Kreplachs are also excellent as an appetizer served crisp and brown.

Ditali, Ham and Cheddar Dinner

UNITED STATES   Serves 6

8 tablespoons of butter
4 tablespoons of flour
2½ cups of light cream
1 teaspoon of salt
⅛ teaspoon of nutmeg
2½ cups of ditali (macaroni cut in very
      short lengths), cooked very
      al dente, drained

2½ cups of ham, cut into small dices
2 cups of grated Cheddar cheese,
      very sharp
2 small white onions, minced
¼ cup of breadcrumbs

In a large saucepan, melt 4 tablespoons of butter; stir in the flour, and cook, stirring, over medium heat, until the paste is smooth and golden. Off heat, slowly pour in the cream, and stir into a smooth mixture. Reduce heat to low, add salt and nutmeg to the sauce in the saucepan and simmer, stirring, for 3 minutes or until it begins to thicken. Stir in the cooked ditali, the ham, 1½ cups of the cheese, and the onion. Butter a 3-quart casserole, pour in the pasta-ham-cheese mixture. Melt the remaining butter and blend it with the remaining cheese and breadcrumbs. Spread this evenly on top of the casserole and cook, uncovered, in a preheated 375-degree oven for 20 minutes or until brown and bubbling.

A Neapolitan Lasagne

ITALY   Serves 6

¾ pound of lasagne
2 tablespoons of olive oil
½ pound of Italian sausage meat
2 cups (about 1½ pounds) of ricotta
  cheese
¼ cup of finely crumbled Gorgonzola
  cheese

1½ cups of freshly grated Asiago or
  Parmesan cheese
2 eggs
¼ teaspoon of nutmeg
Salt and pepper to taste
4 cups of Filetto Sauce (page 206)
2 small mozzarella cheeses, thinly
  sliced

Cook the lasagne in boiling salted water with the olive oil (about 15 minutes), then remove the pasta and lay it on a slightly damp dish towel to drain. While the lasagne is cooking, sauté the sausage meat in a frypan over medium heat for 10 minutes, breaking it up as it cooks. Spoon it into a strainer over a bowl until all the fat drains off. In a bowl, beat the ricotta, Gorgonzola, 1 cup of Asiago or Parmesan, the eggs, nutmeg, salt, and pepper with a fork until well blended. Spread a thin layer of the Filetto Sauce over the bottom of a baking dish. Arrange a layer of lasagne, each one slightly overlapping the next, on the sauce, sprinkle a little of the sausage meat over it, dot with the ricotta mixture, lay a few slices of the mozzarella on top, then spoon some of the Filetto Sauce over all. Continue layering until all of the ingredients are used; but save enough lasagne and sauce to cover the top layer of lasagne completely with sauce. Sprinkle the remaining cheese on top. Bake in a preheated 350-degree oven for 30 minutes, or until the sauce is bubbling.

Roast Leg of Lamb with Orzo

GREECE   Serves 6

1 five-pound leg of lamb
3 large garlic cloves ⎤
1 teaspoon of oregano ⎟
Pinch of thyme   ⎬ mashed together
1 teaspoon of salt   ⎟
½ teaspoon of pepper ⎦
Juice of 1 lemon ⎤
                          ⎬ mixed together
½ cup of olive oil ⎦
2 medium-sized white onions,
coarsely chopped

1 cup of hot water
1 pound of kritharaki (or orzo),
cooked very *al dente,* drained
1 cup of tomato sauce or tomato
purée
Grated Kefalotiri (a salty, Greek,
grating cheese) or Parmesan or
finely crumbled Feta cheese

Place the lamb on a rack in a roasting pan, skin side up. With your hands rub the leg of lamb with the garlic mixture. Spoon some of the lemon juice-oil mixture over the lamb. Sprinkle the onions around the lamb and pour ½ cup of water over the onions. Cook the lamb, uncovered, in a preheated 450-degree oven for 20 minutes. Reduce the heat to 350 degrees. Spoon the remaining lemon juice-oil mixture over the lamb and the remaining water over the onions. Continue to cook for 40 to 60 minutes (depending upon how pink, or well done, you like your lamb), basting occasionally. Transfer the lamb to a hot serving dish and keep warm. Pour off most of the fat in the roasting pan (do not lose any of the onions). Stir in the tomato sauce (or purée), mixing well with the onions. Stir in the kritharaki (or orzo) and return the pan, uncovered, to the oven for about 10 minutes, or until the pasta has absorbed the sauce. Taste for seasoning. Spoon the kritharaki (or orzo) around the lamb and serve. Pass the cheese at the table to sprinkle over the pasta.

Soup-Lamb-and-Vegetable Dinner in One

GREECE   Serves 6

1 tablespoon of olive oil
2 tablespoons of butter
3 pounds of lean lamb, shoulder or
    leg, cut into 1½-inch cubes
1 garlic clove, minced
½ teaspoon of dry oregano
    Salt and pepper to taste
1 cup of dry white wine
4 or 5 cups of chicken broth
3 medium-sized potatoes, peeled and
    halved

12 small white onions, peeled, root
    ends scored
6 small carrots, scraped, cut into
    quarters
1 large celery rib, scraped, cut into
    ¼-inch cubes
2 small zucchini (1 inch by 4 inches),
    each cut into 6 pieces
1 cup of kritharaki (or orzo, fides or
    vermicelli) or other small pasta
2 eggs, separated
    Juice of 1 lemon

In a flameproof casserole, over medium heat, heat the oil and butter. Add the lamb, garlic, oregano; sprinkle with salt and pepper, and brown the lamb. Pour off any fat. Pour in the wine and enough chicken broth to barely cover the lamb. Place in a preheated 350-degree oven, covered, and cook for 25 minutes. Add the potatoes, onions, carrots, and celery, and cook for 20 minutes. Add the zucchini and cook for 10 minutes or until the meat and vegetables are tender. Taste for seasoning. With a slotted spoon, remove the lamb and vegetables, place them on a serving dish and keep them hot. Strain the liquid in the casserole. Return it to the pot and add enough broth to have 5 cups of liquid. Bring it to a boil on top of the stove. Add the pasta and cook about 10 minutes, or until it is *al dente*. In a bowl beat the egg whites until stiff. Add the yolks, beat until blended, then slowly add and beat in the lemon juice. Gradually stir in about 1 cup of the hot broth from the casserole. Return this to the pot, stirring rapidly until well mixed. Serve this lemon-juice–egg–broth–pasta soup first, then serve the meat and vegetables.

Iberian Macaroni and Cheese

SPAIN   Serves 4 to 6

Macaroni and cheese devotees are legion. Here's a tasty version we have had in Madrid.

3 tablespoons of butter
2 ounces of smoked ham, chopped
2 chorizo sausages, skinned, chopped
2 cups of tomato sauce

1 pound of penne rigate (short, pasta tubes), cooked very *al dente*, drained
¾ cup of grated Asiago or Parmesan cheese
1 tablespoon of butter

In a large saucepan (one that will hold the cooked pasta, tomato sauce, and meat) over medium heat, melt the butter and cook the ham and sausage for 10 minutes. Stir in the tomato sauce and the cooked pasta; cook 5 minutes. In a buttered baking dish, place a layer of the pasta and meat mixture, sprinkle with cheese, arrange another layer, sprinkle with cheese, fleck with butter. Cook, uncovered, in a preheated 350-degree oven for 10 minutes, or until brown and bubbling.

Paul Ranieri's Meatballs Fantastic

ITALY   Serves 4 to 6

Paul Ranieri is from the famous Ranieri family of Rome that has kept its restaurant's doors open for more than one hundred years. Paul's base may be the Midwest but his touch is talented and venerable Italian. This is our variation of his recipe:

½ pound of ground top round of beef
½ pound of ground choice chuck
½ pound of ground veal
½ pound of ground lean pork
2 teaspoons of salt
1 teaspoon of pepper
2 tablespoons of broadleaf parsley, minced
2 eggs, beaten
½ cup of fine breadcrumbs
2 large chicken livers, each cut into three pieces, sautéed in butter 2 minutes, until still pink inside

1 large clove of garlic, peeled, cut into slivers
6 pieces of mozzarella cheese, the size of a quarter, but ¼ inch thick
3 tablespoons of olive oil
4 cups of Filetto Sauce (page 206)
12 ounces of penne rigate (pasta tubes cut diagonally at both ends and grooved), cooked *al dente*, drained
½ cup of grated Asiago or Parmesan cheese

In a large bowl, combine the round and chuck beef, the veal, pork, salt, pepper, parsley, eggs, and breadcrumbs. Blend well and form into 6 meatballs about the size of tennis balls. Carefully break the meatballs open and insert in the center of each a piece of the sautéed chicken liver, 1 sliver of garlic, and 1 piece of mozarella cheese. Reform into balls. In a large saucepan, heat the oil and evenly brown the meatballs. Pour off the oil and pour in the Filetto Sauce. Bring to a boil then a simmer and cook for 25 minutes. Serve the meatballs in the center of a ring of the pasta which has been tossed with sauce and sprinkled with cheese.

Spaghetti and Meatballs with a Variation

UNITED STATES   Serves 4 to 6

The offering of meatballs and spaghetti as a main course seems to be primarily American. Although it was probably introduced by Italian-Americans, it is strictly a new-country dish in the same category as chop suey, which originated in Boston, not China. Nevertheless, both dishes have become minor classics.

2 **white onions,** minced
½ **pound of ground beef chuck**
½ **pound of ground round of beef**
1 **egg,** beaten
1 **tablespoon of chopped broadleaf
 parsley**
1½ **teaspoons of Lawry's seasoned salt**
1 **teaspoon of pepper**
½ **cup of fine breadcrumbs**
3 **tablespoons of olive oil**

2 **garlic cloves, chopped**
1 **two-pound can of tomatoes,** put
 through the food mill
½ **teaspoon of dry oregano**
½ **teaspoon of dry basil**
1 **teaspoon of salt**
1 **pound of spaghetti,** cooked
 al dente, drained
½ **cup of grated Asiago or Parmesan
 cheese**

Cook the onions in butter and save the butter. In a bowl, combine the ground meats, egg, parsley, Lawry's salt, ½ teaspoon of pepper, the onions (with the butter, in which they cooked) and the breadcrumbs. Mix well and form into balls the size of golf balls. In a large pot, heat the oil and brown the meatballs evenly. Remove. In the same pot, cook the garlic until soft. Add the tomatoes, oregano, basil, salt, and ½ teaspoon of pepper. Stir well. Cook, uncovered, at a simmer, for 25 minutes. Add the meatballs and cook for another 20 minutes, or until the sauce is smooth and thickened.

Toss one-half of the sauce with the hot cooked pasta. Serve on a large platter, with the remainder of the sauce spooned on top of the pasta, ringed by meatballs, or on individual warm plates, dividing the pasta and meatballs evenly among guests. Pass the cheese at the table.

VARIATION

For unique meatballs, follow the same recipe but form each meatball with a large nugget of Gorgonzola cheese in its center.

Meatballs and Vermicelli

HOLLAND   Serves 6

¼ cup of ground veal
¼ cup of ground pork
½ teaspoon of salt
½ teaspoon of pepper
⅛ teaspoon of nutmeg

1 egg, beaten
Flour for dredging meatballs
8 cups of beef broth
1 cup of vermicelli, broken into
   ¼-inch pieces

In a bowl, place the veal, pork, salt, pepper, nutmeg, and egg. Blend well and shape into small balls about ½ inch in diameter. Dredge lightly with flour. In a pot, bring the beef broth to a boil, reduce to a simmer; add the meatballs and simmer for 10 minutes. Add the vermicelli and simmer for 10 minutes or until the vermicelli is cooked. Taste for seasoning.

Spaghetti Vagdalthussal

HUNGARY   Serves 4

2 tablespoons of butter
1 pound of ground lean pork
2 tablespoons of chopped broadleaf
   parsley
1 pound of spaghetti, cooked very
   al dente, drained

3 tablespoons of hot bacon fat (or
   substitute melted butter, but try
   for bacon fat)
1 cup of grated Romano cheese
½ cup of sour cream

In a saucepan, melt the butter and cook the pork for 15 minutes. Stir in the parsley. Toss the cooked spaghetti in the hot bacon fat. Butter a baking dish or casserole and arrange alternate layers of spaghetti, meat, and cheese, ending with spaghetti. Cover with the sour cream and bake, uncovered, in a preheated 325-degree oven for 30 minutes, or until bubbling and brown.

Pasta Meat Pockets

POLAND   Serves 4

2 cups of flour
2 small eggs, beaten
2 tablespoons of warm water
2 cups of cooked beef, finely
   chopped
2 slices of dry bread, broken into
   small pieces

¼ cup of milk
Salt and pepper to taste
1 tablespoon of butter
1 medium-sized onion, minced
4 tablespoons of butter, melted
½ cup of grated Asiago or Parmesan
   cheese

In a bowl, place the flour, eggs, and water; work into a firm, smooth dough. Form into a ball and let set, covered, while you make the filling. In a bowl, blend the beef, bread, milk, salt, and pepper. In a saucepan, melt the butter and cook the onion until soft. Spoon this into the bowl with the beef and blend well. On a floured pastry board, roll the dough (divided into 4 balls) into sheets no more than ⅛ of an inch thick. Cut into 3-inch squares. Place a heaping teaspoon of the beef mixture in the center of each square of dough. Moisten the inside edges of each square with water, then fold them into triangles, pressing the sides firmly together. In a large pot, bring 3 quarts of water to the boil, add 1 tablespoon of salt, reduce water to a simmer; lower the filled squares into it and cook until the "pockets" rise to the surface. Drain on paper towels; place on a serving dish, drench with the melted butter, and sprinkle meat pockets with the grated cheese. Good as a lunch, or served with a clear beef broth.

Noodle Mix-Up

UNITED STATES   Serves 6

Americans are often good at adapting recipes to suit their own tastes. Here is an adaption of an original Italian recipe from Joyce Livingston, of Wichita, Kansas.

2 tablespoons of olive oil
1 large onion, chopped
1 garlic clove, minced
¾ pound of bulk sausage
1¾ pounds of ground chuck beef
1 celery rib, scraped and chopped
1 tablespoon of chopped parsley
1 two-pound can of tomatoes, run
   through the food mill

1 pound of egg noodles, cooked
   al dente, drained
1 ten-ounce package of frozen peas,
   defrosted
1 eight and a half-ounce can of
   whole kernel corn
10 green olives, sliced

In a large pot, heat the oil and sauté the onion and garlic until soft; add the sausage meat, ground beef, celery, parsley and tomatoes; cook over medium heat, stirring, for 20 minutes. Add the noodles, peas, corn, and olives, blending well. Simmer for 5 minutes.

Goreng Noodles

INDONESIA   Serves 4

4 tablespoons of peanut oil
2 small onions, chopped
3 garlic cloves, minced
1 red chili pepper, seeded, thinly
   sliced
½ teaspoon of dried shrimp paste
1 pound of lean pork, cut into tiny
   cubes
½ pound of shrimp, shelled, deveined

1 large celery rib, scraped, thinly
   sliced
¼ head of a small cabbage, shredded
Salt and pepper to taste
½ pound of very fine noodles, cooked
   very *al dente*, drained
2 tablespoons of soy sauce
3 scallions, chopped

In a frypan, heat the peanut oil and cook the onions, garlic, and pepper until they are soft. Stir in the shrimp paste and pork, and cook, stirring, for 15 minutes. Add the shrimp, celery, cabbage, salt, and pepper, and cook, stirring, for 5 minutes. Stir in the noodles, blend well, and cook for 5 minutes. Sprinkle with the soy sauce. Serve on a hot platter with the scallions sprinkled on top.

Noodles with Ground Meat

HUNGARY   Serves 6

2 tablespoons of butter
1 pound of ground veal
½ pound of ground lean pork
  Salt to taste
2 tablespoons of chopped broadleaf
  parsley
2 teaspoons of Hungarian paprika

2 tablespoons of hot bacon fat
1 pound of capellini (very fine
  noodles), cooked very al dente,
  (it could be in seconds), drained
½ cup of grated Romano cheese
½ cup of sour cream

In a saucepan, melt the butter, add the meat, sprinkle with salt, and brown. Off heat, stir in the parsley and paprika. In another saucepan, place the bacon fat and stir the cooked noodles into it, blending well. In a buttered baking dish, alternate layers of noodles and meat, sprinkling cheese on each layer. Cover the top evenly with the sour cream and bake, uncovered, in a preheated 375-degree oven for 30 minutes or until brown and bubbling.

Soft Fried Rice Noodles with Shrimp and Pork

CHINA   Serves 6

4 tablespoons of peanut oil
4 whole scallions, cut on the diagonal
  in ½-inch pieces
½ pound of lean pork, cut into strips
  1-by-½-by-½ inch thick
¼ cup of dried shrimp, soaked in
  warm water for 30 minutes,
  drained
1 tablespoon of soy sauce
3 dried, black Chinese mushrooms,
  soaked in warm water for 30
  minutes, drained, squeezed dry,
  stems removed, caps shredded

¼ cup of shredded bamboo shoots
¼ cup of thinly sliced water chestnuts
¼ cup of preserved tea melon,
  drained, cut in ½-inch-long
  pieces
2 tablespoons of chicken broth
1 pound of rice noodles, boiled for
  7 minutes, drained, rinsed
  under cold water, and mixed
  with 1 tablespoon of peanut oil

In a wok or saucepan, heat 2 tablespoons of peanut oil over medium heat and stir-fry the scallions for 35 seconds. Add the pork, and stir-fry for 2 to 3 minutes, or until the pink color is gone. Stir in the shrimp, cook 25 seconds. Stir in the soy sauce, mushrooms, bamboo shoots, and water chestnuts; stir-fry for 1 minute. Add the tea melon and chicken broth; stir-fry for 1 minute. In another wok or saucepan, heat the remaining oil and stir-fry the noodles for 1½ minutes, or until thoroughly heated. Add to the other wok or saucepan and blend well, tossing gently.

Pastitso

GREECE   Serves 8 to 10

This is classic, a tasty combination of layers of spicy ground meat, macaroni, a Greek or Italian grating cheese of your choice, and a rich cream sauce.

STEP 1. THE CREAM SAUCE

6 tablespoons of butter
4 tablespoons of flour
3 cups of light cream
1 cup of chicken broth

½ cup grated Kefalotiri or Parmesan
    cheese
Salt and pepper to taste

In a saucepan melt the butter, gradually stir in the flour, and cook, stirring, until you have a smooth, thick paste. Stir in the cream and broth, a
small amount at a time, stirring constantly until the sauce is medium thick
and smooth. Stir in the grated cheese, salt, and pepper, and heat until the
cheese has melted.

STEP 2. THE MEAT LAYER

2 tablespoons of butter
2 medium-sized onions, chopped
2 pounds of chopped chuck beef, or
    1 pound of beef and 1 pound
    of sausage meat
½ teaspoon of cinnamon

½ teaspoon of nutmeg
½ teaspoon of allspice
Salt and pepper to taste
1 cup of thick tomato paste
¼ cup of white wine

In a frypan, cook the onions in the butter until they are soft. Add the beef
(or whatever meat you are using), breaking it up with a fork, cooking until
it is well browned. Drain fat from the pan and stir in the cinnamon, nutmeg,
allspice, salt, pepper, tomato sauce, and wine. Simmer, uncovered, 15 minutes. Set aside.

STEP 3. THE MACARONI

1 pound of elbow macaroni or ziti broken into 1½-inch pieces cooked very *al dente* and drained	**¾ cup of grated Kefalotiri or Parmesan cheese**
3 eggs	**2 tablespoons of very soft butter**

Beat together the eggs, one-half cup of the grated cheese and all of the butter, then mix well with the macaroni.

To assemble: Spoon one-half of the macaroni mixture in a buttered 9-by-13-inch baking dish. Spoon some of the cream sauce over it. Spoon all of the meat mixture over the macaroni. Spoon some of the cream sauce over it. Spoon the remaining macaroni over the meat layer, and pour the remaining cream sauce over it. Sprinkle with the remaining ¼ cup of cheese. Bake in a preheated 350-degree oven for 45 minutes, until bubbling. Cool 15 minutes; cut into 3-inch squares and serve.

Lebanese Pasta Pilaf

Serves 4

Middle Easterners, especially the Lebanese, like to mix rice with pasta and serve a savory dish such as lamb and peas (below) on top of the mixture.

PASTA AND RICE

1 stick (¼ pound) of butter	**1 cup of long-grain rice**
1 medium-sized onion, minced	**2 cups of chicken broth**
½ cup of vermicelli, broken into 1-inch pieces	**1 teaspoon of salt**

In a saucepan, melt the butter, and over medium heat cook the onion until soft. Add the vermicelli and cook for 2 minutes. Stir in the rice, and cook 3 minutes, coating it and the pasta well with the butter. Add the broth and the salt; cover the pan and simmer for 20 minutes or until the pasta and rice have absorbed all of the liquid. Fluff with a fork.

LAMB WITH PEAS

3 tablespoons of butter
2 tablespoons of olive oil
1 pound of lean lamb, cut into 1-inch
   cubes
2 medium-sized white onions,
   finely chopped
1 teaspoon of dry mint leaves
1 teaspoon of dry tarragon leaves

2 cups of chicken broth
1½ teaspoons of salt
½ teaspoon of pepper
Juice of half a lemon
2 cups of fresh shelled peas, cooked
   in a small amount of water until
   almost tender, yet still firm (or
   frozen peas, defrosted)

In a pot, heat 1 tablespoon of butter and the oil. Add the lamb, onion, mint, and tarragon; cover and cook over medium heat for 15 minutes or until the lamb has browned, stirring frequently. Stir in the broth, salt, and pepper, and cook for 40 minutes, covered, or until the lamb is fork-tender. Add the lemon juice, peas and the remaining butter; cook until the peas are tender and serve over the pasta-pilaf.

Rumanian Pork with Noodles

Serves 6

5 eggs
2 teaspoons of salt
1 pound of fine noodles, cooked
   very *al dente*, drained
2 medium-thick slices of white
   bread, crusts removed, broken
   into small pieces and blended
   in a large bowl with ½ cup of
   light cream
1½ pounds of lean pork, ground

1 medium-sized white onion,
   chopped
½ teaspoon of dried oregano
1 teaspoon of salt
½ teaspoon of pepper
3 tablespoons of chopped
   broad-leaf parsley
1 stick of sweet butter, cut into small
   pieces
½ cup of sour cream
½ cup of grated provolone

In a bowl, beat 3 of the eggs with the salt, and gently stir in the noodles until they are coated with the egg. Reserve. Into the same bowl in which the bread and cream have been blended, add the pork, onion, oregano, salt, pepper and parsley. Mix well with your hands, then beat with a spoon until it is smooth and light. Butter a large casserole and arrange one-third of the noodles across the bottom. Evenly spoon half of the pork mixture over the noodles, making a smooth layer. Sprinkle with one-third of the pieces of butter. Spread half of the remaining noodles on top and cover them with the rest of the meat mixture; sprinkle another one-third of the butter over the meat layer, and add the last of the noodles. Dot with the remaining butter. Cover, and cook in a preheated 400-degree oven for 35 minutes.

In a small bowl, beat the remaining 2 eggs, the sour cream and the cheese until well blended. Pour over the pork-noodle mixture, and cover the casserole; cook for 30 minutes. Remove the cover and cook for another 20 minutes or until brown and bubbling. Rumanians unmold their dish by running a table knife along the insides of the casserole, placing an inverted serving plate on top, then turning the casserole upside down on the plate.

Pork Strips and Pasta

CHINA   Serves 6

2 **pounds of pork loin,** cut into
   thin strips
2 **tablespoons peanut oil**
1 **cup of chicken broth**
5 **scallions,** minced
½ **teaspoon of salt**

½ **teaspoon of black pepper**
3 **tablespoons of cornstarch**
4 **teaspoons of soy sauce**
½ **cup water**
1 **pound of narrow egg noodles,**
   cooked *al dente,* drained

Sauté the pork strips in oil until browned, add broth and scallions; season with salt and pepper. Cover; simmer for 20 minutes. Blend the cornstarch, soy sauce, and water; add to the pork pan. Taste for seasoning. Stir until the sauce thickens. Serve over the hot noodles.

Jim Anelli's Farfalle with Pot Roast Sauce

ITALY   Serves 6

1 large garlic clove
2 tablespoons of broadleaf parsley
¼ cup of chopped salt pork
1 two-pound piece of lean pork loin
   or top round of beef
5 tablespoons of butter
3 tablespoons of olive oil
   Salt and pepper to taste
3 medium-sized yellow onions,
   finely chopped
1 medium-sized carrot, scraped and
   finely chopped

1 celery rib, scraped and finely
   chopped
½ teaspoon of dried oregano
½ teaspoon of dried basil
   Pinch of dried red-pepper flakes
¾ cup of dry, red wine
½ cup of tomato purée
1 one-pound, twelve-ounce can of
   tomatoes, put through a food
   mill
1 pound of farfalle ("butterflies")
   Parmesan cheese

Chop the garlic, parsley, and salt pork together, making a paste. Make a few incisions in the meat and fill them with the paste. In a casserole, over medium heat, heat 2 tablespoons of butter and 1 tablespoon of oil. Add the meat, sprinkle with salt and pepper, and brown it evenly. Remove the meat. Pour the fat from the casserole. Heat 2 tablespoons of oil in the casserole. Add the onions, carrot, and celery. Cook 5 minutes or until the vegetables are soft. Stir in the oregano, basil, red-pepper flakes, wine, tomato purée, and tomatoes, and simmer for about 10 minutes, stirring occasionally. Return the meat to the casserole, cover, and cook in a preheated 300-degree oven for 2½ hours, or until the meat is tender. Spoon off the fat that collects on the top. Taste the sauce for seasoning. Cook the farfalle in boiling salted water until *al dente*. Drain well. Mix it with the remaining butter in a warm bowl. Serve in hot rimmed soup bowls with the sauce spooned on top. Pass the cheese at the table, and serve the pot roast after the pasta.

Russian Ravioli

Makes about 2 pounds

This is a Siberian specialty called *pelmeni*, rounds of dough with a meat filling. In the frigid Siberian climate, they are made by the thousands, placed on floured boards, carried outdoors to freeze, then packed in sacks and stored. The fillings range from a mixture of beef and pork (the favorite, below) through cabbage, mushroom, mushroom and egg, fish, radish (another favorite), and various other vegetables, mutton, and cheese.

DOUGH

4½ cups of flour
1½ teaspoons of salt

3 eggs
1 cup of water, more or less

In a bowl, place the flour and salt, and form a well in the center of the mound of flour. Add the eggs and two-thirds of the water to the well, mixing in completely, and adding more water, if necessary, to make a ball of dough soft enough to knead. Place the dough ball on a lightly-floured pastry board and knead it with your hands, forming it into a thick sheet, folding and refolding it end to end. Using pressure, place the heel of the hand on the dough pushing down and forward. Knead until the dough is smooth and flexible. Reform it into a ball; wrap it loosely with waxed paper and set aside for 2 hours.

BEEF AND PORK STUFFING

3 tablespoons of butter
1 tablespoon of olive oil
3 medium-sized white onions, finely chopped
1 pound of beef chuck, finely chopped

½ pound of pork fatback, finely chopped
1½ teaspoons of salt
½ teaspoon of pepper
½ cup of beef broth

In a saucepan, heat the butter and oil and sauté the onions for 5 minutes. Stir in the beef, pork fatback, salt, pepper, and beef broth, and cook for 10 minutes, blending into a smooth mixture. Cool. On a lightly-floured pastry board, roll out the dough to a ⅛ inch thickness, thinner if you can manage it. With a 2½-inch cookie cutter, cut out rounds. Place about ½ teaspoon of the meat stuffing on the lower half of each round of dough. Dip a finger in cold water and run it around the edges of the dough. Fold into half-moon pouches and seal the edges by pressing with the back side of the prongs of a fork. Bring 3 quarts of water to a boil. Cook about 10 pelmeni at a time, reducing the water to a simmer as you cook them for about 10 minutes, or until they float to the surface. The Russians serve them in clear soup or as a side dish with hot melted butter, sour cream, or butter and vinegar, and sometimes just with a topping of chopped green onions.

Farmer's Sausage and Gemelli

GERMANY   Serves 6

½ pound of gemelli (pasta "twins"), cooked very *al dente*, drained
1 ten-ounce package of tiny frozen peas, thawed
3 tablespoons of melted butter
1 ten-ounce package of spinach (fresh or frozen), cooked, drained

1 pound of German Farmer's Sausage (or frank- furters), sliced
1 ten and a half-ounce can of cream of mushroom soup
½ cup of sour cream
½ cup of milk
Salt and pepper to taste
} blended
6 slices of bacon, cooked, drained of fat, crumbled

In a bowl, place the cooked pasta, half of the peas, and the melted butter; blend. Butter a large baking dish, layer it with the spinach. Arrange the pasta and peas mixture evenly over the spinach. Pour the blended mixture of sausage, soup, sour cream, and milk over the pasta and peas layer. Bake, uncovered, in a preheated 400-degree oven for 20 minutes. Sprinkle the remaining peas and the bacon on top. Cook another 8 minutes or until bubbling and brown.

Baked Ditali with Sweet and Hot Italian Sausages

ITALY   Serves 6

"Ditali," meaning "thimbles" in Italian, is a curved pasta, cut into short lengths. This is a welcome and easy-to-make change from lasagna. The pairing of sausages here is a taste-bud treat.

1 tablespoon of olive oil
1 pound of sweet Italian sausages
1 pound of hot Italian sausages
4 cups of tomato sauce (commercial or your own)

1½ pounds of ditali (very short, hollow pasta), cooked very *al dente* (quite chewy), drained
1½ cups of ricotta cheese
1 cup of grated Parmesan cheese

In a saucepan, heat the oil and brown the sausages evenly. Remove the sausages, cut them into thin slices. Pour the oil out of the pan but leave the brown residue. Add the tomato sauce to the same pan, add the sausage slices; stir, cover, and simmer 20 minutes. Butter a baking dish and spoon a layer of the cooked drained ditali evenly across the bottom, cover with a layer of sausage slices in tomato sauce. Then spread with a layer of ricotta, sprinkled with Parmesan. Repeat the layering until the pasta, sausages, and cheese are used, ending with a layer of sauce and cheese. Bake, uncovered, in a preheated 350-degree oven for 25 minutes or until sauce is bubbling. Serve in individual, warm plates.

Spaetzle Baked with Ham

GERMANY   Serves 4 to 6

4 tablespoons of butter
1 medium-sized onion, chopped
6 medium-sized fresh, white
   mushrooms, sliced
2 tablespoons of sherry
  Salt and pepper to taste

1 recipe of spaetzle, cooked and
   drained (page 11)
8 thin slices of Westphalian, prosciutto, or a good boiled ham,
   cut into 2-inch squares
½ cup of breadcrumbs, mixed with
   2 tablespoons of melted butter

In a frypan, melt 2 tablespoons of butter. Add the onion and cook until soft. Add the remaining butter and the mushrooms and cook for 2 minutes. Stir in the sherry, and season with salt and pepper. In a buttered baking dish, arrange a layer of spaetzle, and spoon over it one-half of the mushrooms and onion mixture. Arrange the ham squares over the mushrooms and onions, and layer with the remaining spaetzle; spoon the remaining mushroom and onion mixture over that. Sprinkle the dish with the buttered breadcrumbs and place it in a preheated 400-degree oven for 30 minutes, or until heated through and the crumbs are brown.

Macaroni with Spareribs

CUBA   Serves 6 to 8

2 tablespoons of achiote lard
3 ounces of lean salt pork, chopped
2 sweet chili peppers, seeded,
    chopped
½ cup of tomato sauce
1 pound of lean spareribs, cut into
    individual ribs
1 teaspoon of salt
6 green olives, pitted, chopped

6 black olives, pitted, chopped
1 cup of dry red wine
1 pound of elbow macaroni, cooked
    very *al dente*, drained
1 one-pound can of whole bell
    tomatoes
½ cup of grated Asiago or Parmesan
    cheese

In a large pot, melt the lard and sauté the salt pork and peppers for 5 minutes. Stir in the tomato sauce, add the spareribs, salt, olives, and red wine, cover and cook over low heat for 1 hour, or until the spareribs are almost tender. Taste the sauce for seasoning. Stir in the cooked macaroni and the canned tomatoes; cover, and simmer for 20 minutes. Serve sprinkled with the grated cheese.

Sformato (Timbale) di Bucatini

ITALY   Serves 4 to 6

2 cups of flour
1 teaspoon of salt
6 tablespoons of butter
1 small lightly beaten egg
1 small eggplant, peeled, salted, and
  let stand for half an hour
2 tablespoons of olive oil
  Meatballs about ½-inch in diameter
  made from ½ pound of ground
  beef (use your favorite meatball
  recipe)
Salt and pepper to taste

½ pound of bucatini (a hollow pasta
  smaller than macaroni), broken
  into 2-inch lengths, cooked very
  al dente, and drained
2 tablespoons of cooked ham, cut in
  julienne style
1 cup of Filetto Sauce (page 206)
½ cup of mozzarella cheese in small
  dices
¼ cup of grated Asiago or Parmesan
  cheese
3 tablespoons of beef broth

Make a pastry with the flour, salt, butter, and egg. Roll out two-thirds of
the dough and line a 3-inch-deep mold or a deep pie plate. Cut the eggplant
into small cubes, sauté them in 1 tablespoon of the oil until golden. Season
with salt and pepper. Remove with a slotted spoon, drain on paper towels,
and keep warm. Add remaining oil to the pan you cooked the eggplant in,
and brown the meatballs, seasoning them with salt and pepper. Combine
the eggplant, meatballs, bucatini, ham, filetto sauce, and the cheeses. Fill the
mold with this mixture and spoon in the broth. Roll out the remaining pastry,
cover the filling with this. Press the edges together. Prick the top in several
places and bake in a preheated 425-degree oven for ½ hour or until golden.
Serve as it is or with a Bolognese sauce (page 117).

Mushroom and Sausage Timbale

FRANCE   Serves 6

1 pound of perciatelli (a hollow
    pasta, larger than spaghetti),
    broken into ½-inch pieces
1½ sticks (12 tablespoons) of butter
1 pound of whole, small mushrooms
    (do not use stems)

Juice of half a lemon
½ cup of water
Salt and pepper to taste
24 tiny pork sausages
½ cup of grated Gruyère or Parmesan
    cheese

Cook the pasta in boiling, salted water until *al dente*. Drain and toss in a hot bowl with 4 tablespoons of butter. Keep warm. In a frypan, heat 3 tablespoons of butter, add the mushrooms, lemon juice, and water. Sprinkle lightly with salt and pepper, and cook over high heat, stirring, until most of the liquid has evaporated. Keep hot. Prick the sausages with the point of a knife and blanch them in hot water for 2 minutes. Drain the sausages, then brown them in 2 tablespoons of butter. Combine the pasta, mushrooms (with whatever juice remains in the pan), the sausages, remaining butter, and the cheese; mix well. Taste for seasoning. Mound on a hot dish and serve.

144

Bursa Dansi (Baked Veal with Pasta)

TURKEY   Serves 6

1 garlic clove, minced
Black pepper
1 teaspoon of salt
1 bay leaf
1 teaspoon of dried tarragon
1 cup of dry white wine
2 pounds of veal steak, boned and
  pounded flat
4 tablespoons of butter

2 tablespoons of olive oil
2 medium-sized onions, minced
2 celery ribs, scraped and chopped
6 medium-sized mushrooms, thinly
  sliced
4 ripe tomatoes, skinned and diced
1½ cups of yogurt
1 pound of narrow egg noodles,
  cooked very *al dente*, drained

Make a marinade of the garlic, pepper, salt, bay leaf, tarragon, and the wine. Add the veal and marinate it in the refrigerator for 5 hours, turning after 2 hours. Drain, pat dry with paper towels, and cut into 1-inch squares. Heat 2 tablespoons of the butter and the olive oil in a frypan and brown the squares of veal. Remove from the pan and keep warm. Add to the pan the remaining butter and sauté the onions and celery until they are soft. Stir in the tomatoes and mushrooms, and simmer, uncovered, stirring frequently for 15 minutes, or until the sauce thickens. Stir in the yogurt and heat thoroughly but do not boil. Taste for seasoning. Mix the noodles with the veal and juices from the veal, and transfer to a buttered, baking dish. Cover with the yogurt and vegetable sauce, and bake, uncovered, in a preheated 400-degree oven for 20 minutes or until the sauce starts to bubble.

VII

Specialty Meats

*T*HESE INDEED ARE "SPECIAL" MEATS, which can add novelty and interest to your entertaining. Despite America's mix of ethnic backgrounds, we have been the slowest of countries to discover the treasures of the table discussed in this chapter. While many of us have progressed to the point where we can eat chicken livers without wincing, few of us would pound the table in delight if we were served tripe, not many would revel in sweet-breads, and some would even balk at being served kidneys. Serve pasta with these specialty meats, however, and you'll hear no protests from your dinner guests. In fact, you'll probably get raves.

In the recipes that follow are the precious morsels that the Old World has respected for generations. We've tried to coax you along by giving liver main billing.

Fusilli Bucati with Baby Beef Liver

CORSICA   Serves 6

3 tablespoons of butter
2 tablespoons of olive oil
2 small white onions, minced
2 small carrots, scraped, minced
1 celery rib, scraped and minced
    Salt and pepper to taste
8 small fresh mushrooms, finely
    chopped
½ cup of Marsala wine

1 cup of beef broth
1 pound of young beef liver, cut into
    ¼-inch-thick slices, then cut
    into narrow 1½-inch strips and
    seasoned with salt and pepper
1 pound of fusilli bucati (thin hollow
    twists), cooked *al dente*, drained
¾ cup of grated Swiss and Parmesan
    cheese mixed

In a saucepan heat 2 tablespoons of butter and 1 of olive oil, and sauté the onions, carrots, and celery for 6 minutes. Season with salt and pepper. Add the mushrooms, sauté for 1 minute. Pour in the Marsala, simmer until evaporated. Stir in the beef broth, and continue to simmer while you cook the liver. In a large frypan, heat the remaining butter and oil, and quickly sauté the seasoned liver strips until brown on the outside. Do not overcook; the liver should be pink inside. Add the liver to the vegetable sauce and blend. In a hot bowl, place the hot cooked pasta, add the vegetable and liver sauce and blend well. Pass the cheese at the table.

Bulgur Wheat and Vermicelli Pilaf with Calf's Liver, Green Peppers and Tomatoes

LEBANON   Serves 4 to 6

THE PILAF

2 tablespoons of olive oil
2 tablespoons of butter
1 medium-sized onion, finely
 chopped
1 cup bulgur wheat

1 cup of vermicelli, broken into
 1-inch pieces
3 cups of hot chicken broth
½ teaspoon of cumin
Salt to taste

In a heavy saucepan, over medium heat, heat the oil and butter. Add the onion, and sauté until it is soft. Add the bulgur wheat and the vermicelli, and stir until they are well coated with butter and oil. Stir in the broth, cumin and salt. Bring the broth to a boil, stir, and on low heat, cook, covered, for 20 minutes, or until the liquid has been absorbed and the wheat and vermicelli are tender. Fluff with a fork. Set aside and keep warm.

2 tablespoons of olive oil
5 tablespoons of butter
1 large garlic clove, minced
1 pound of calf's liver, cut into 2-by-
 1-inch strips and dredged in
 flour seasoned with salt and
 pepper
1 tablespoon of fresh minced mint or
 1 teaspoon of dried mint

1 green pepper, seeds and white part
 removed, cut into ¼-inch strips
2 medium-sized, ripe, but firm,
 tomatoes, cut into ½-inch
 slices
Salt and pepper to taste
3 tablespoons of lemon juice

In a large frypan, over medium heat, heat 1 tablespoon of oil and 2 tablespoons of butter. Stir in the garlic. Add the strips of liver in one layer and sauté for 2 minutes on each side (the liver should be pink inside, brown on the outside). Remove the liver and keep it warm. Add the remaining oil and 1 tablespoon of butter to the frypan, stir in the mint and the pepper strips. Sauté for 2 minutes, stirring. The pepper should be crisp. Arrange the tomato slices in the frypan and sauté for 1 minute on each side. Sprinkle with salt and pepper. Transfer the peppers and tomatoes to the liver dish. Add the lemon juice and remaining butter to the frypan; stir and heat to a simmer. On a large warm serving dish, mound the pilaf, arrange the liver, peppers and tomatoes on and around the pilaf, spoon the lemon juice sauce over all and serve.

Spaetzle with Sweet and Sour Calf's Liver

ISRAEL   Serves 4

3 tablespoons of chicken fat (or
  vegetable oil)
3 medium-sized white onions, thinly
  sliced
1 pound of calf's liver, sliced ¼ inch
  thick, then cut into narrow,
  1½-inch strips
2 tablespoons of flour

½ teaspoon of paprika
  Salt and pepper to taste
1 cup of boiling water
3 tablespoons of fresh lemon juice
2 teaspoons of sugar
2 cups of hot, cooked spaetzle
  (page 11)

In a saucepan, heat the chicken fat (or oil) and cook the onions 5 minutes, or until soft. Stir in the liver strips, sprinkle with flour and paprika, season with salt and pepper and cook 4 minutes. Liver should be lightly browned, but very pink inside. Do not overcook, as it has more cooking to do. Stir in the boiling water, lemon juice, and sugar; cook, stirring, for 5 minutes or until the sauce has thickened. Serve spooned over hot spaetzle.

Penne Rigate with Lamb Kidneys

PORTUGAL   Serves 6

6 lamb kidneys
6 tablespoons of butter
1 small celery rib, scraped and
    minced
1 garlic clove, minced
    Salt and pepper to taste
2 tablespoons of flour

1½ cups of chicken broth
2 tablespoons of dry sherry
¾ cup of heavy cream
1 pound of penne rigate (grooved
    pasta quills), cooked *al dente*,
    drained
2 tablespoons of chopped parsley

Trim the outer membranes from the kidneys and cut the fat and inner white membrane out with a scissors. In a frypan, over medium heat, melt 3 tablespoons of butter. Add the celery and garlic, and sauté for 3 minutes, or until the celery is soft. Add the kidneys, sprinkle with salt and pepper, and over high heat sauté them 5 minutes or until the outside is brown and the inside still pink. Test by cutting into one with a knife. Transfer the kidneys to a hot bowl, cover and keep warm. Stir the flour into the frypan, mixing it well with the contents of the pan. Gradually add the chicken broth, stirring into a smooth sauce. Stir in the sherry and the cream, and simmer 3 minutes, or until the sauce slightly thickens. Taste for seasoning. Cut the kidneys into ⅛-inch-thick slices, add them to the sauce and simmer 2 minutes or until they are heated through. Place the pasta in a hot bowl with the remaining 3 tablespoons of butter. Mix with half of the sauce. Spoon into hot rimmed soup bowls and spoon the remaining sauce on top; sprinkle with parsley.

Lasagnette Mold with Veal Kidneys

GREAT BRITAIN   Serves 6

THE MOLD

12 ounces of lasagnette (wide
    noodles), cooked very *al dente*,
    drained
4 tablespoons of butter
1½ tablespoons of flour
1½ cups of light cream, warmed

½ cup of grated double Gloucester
    (or Gruyère) cheese
Salt and pepper to taste
2 egg yolks, beaten
3 tablespoons of fine breadcrumbs

While the pasta is cooking, make the sauce. In a saucepan, melt the butter and add the flour; stirring into a smooth paste. Gradually add the warm cream, stirring and simmering over low heat until the sauce is smooth and thickened. Add the cheese and stir until melted. Season to taste with salt and pepper. Remove from the heat, cool slightly, and stir in the beaten egg yolks, blending into a smooth sauce. In a bowl, toss the hot, cooked pasta with the sauce and blend well. Butter a deep 9-inch oven mold with a 3-inch center well and dust it with the breadcrumbs, shaking out any excess crumbs; pour the noodle mixture into it. Set this in a pan of hot water and cook in a preheated 400-degree oven for 15 minutes or until set.

THE FILLING

½ pound of veal kidneys, trimmed,
    diced
3 tablespoons of butter
1 tablespoon of flour

Salt and pepper to taste
2 ounces of sherry
1 cup of chicken broth
½ pound of fresh mushrooms, sliced

While the pasta ring is in the oven, prepare the filling for it. In a saucepan sauté the kidneys in the butter for 5 minutes. Sprinkle with flour, salt, and pepper; stir in the sherry, chicken broth, and mushrooms. Cook, stirring, just until the sauce thickens. Taste for seasoning. The kidneys and mushrooms should not be overcooked. Turn the pasta mold upside down onto a warm serving dish. Fill the center with the kidneys and mushrooms in their sauce

Pasta with Chicken Giblets

SPAIN   Serves 4 to 6

2 tablespoons of butter
1 tablespoon of olive oil
2 medium-sized yellow onions,
    chopped
½ pound of chicken giblets (hearts
    and gizzards), chopped
¾ cup of chopped, uncooked ham
½ cup of tomato purée

1 cup of water
5 ounces of dry white wine
    Salt and pepper to taste
1 pound of elbow macaroni, or ditali,
    cooked very *al dente*, drained
1 cup of grated Asiago or Parmesan
    cheese
2 tablespoons of butter

In saucepan, over medium heat, heat the butter and oil, and cook the onions, giblets, and ham for 10 minutes; stirring. Add the tomato purée, water and wine. Season with salt and pepper, stir well, cover, and simmer for 10 minutes. In a buttered baking dish alternate layers of pasta and giblets in their sauce; sprinkle each layer with cheese, saving one-fourth cup to sprinkle on the top. Fleck with butter, and bake, uncovered, in a preheated 350-degree oven for 20 minutes, or until brown and bubbling.

Gemelli with Chicken Livers

UNITED STATES   Serves 4 to 6

Gemelli, or "twins," look like two short pieces of spaghetti twisted together. It is a unique pasta and a welcome change from spaghetti.

2 tablespoons of cooking oil
½ pound of chicken livers
½ pound of fresh mushrooms, sliced
½ cup of pitted, quartered, black
    olives
⅓ cup of sherry

Salt and pepper to taste
1 pound of gemelli cooked *al dente*,
    drained
½ cup of grated, aged, sharp Cheddar
    cheese

In a saucepan, heat the oil and cook the livers 5 minutes, or until evenly browned, but pink inside. Remove the livers and chop them. In the same saucepan in which the livers cooked, sauté the mushrooms for 4 minutes. Stir in the cooked livers, olives, and sherry. Season with salt and pepper and cook for 3 minutes, stirring well. In a buttered casserole, arrange a layer of the cooked pasta, top with an even layer of the chicken liver mixture, and sprinkle generously with the cheese. Place under a broiler for 3 minutes, or until the cheese has melted and is golden.

Linguine with Chicken Livers

ITALY   Serves 4 to 6

4 tablespoons of olive oil
1 pound of chicken livers, halved
4 small white onions, chopped
2 garlic cloves, chopped
1 teaspoon of dry oregano
½ teaspoon of red-pepper flakes
1 tablespoon of dry basil
1 teaspoon of salt

2 two-pound cans of plum tomatoes with basil leaf (place in a bowl and break into small pieces with your hands)
1 pound of linguine (flat spaghetti), cooked, *al dente*, drained
1 cup of grated Asiago or Parmesan cheese

In a large pot, heat the oil and evenly brown the livers (do not overcook, they should be pink inside). Remove the livers and set aside. Add the onions, garlic, oregano, pepper flakes, basil, and salt to the pot. Stir well, blending. Cook 8 minutes, or until onions are soft. Pour in the tomatoes, stir well, and cook, uncovered, stirring often, for 20 minutes or until the sauce thickens. Add the livers and cook for 5 minutes. Taste for seasoning. In a warm bowl, place several tablespoons of the sauce (without livers), add the pasta, and toss well but gently. Add more sauce, without livers, toss, and serve on hot plates with sauce and livers liberally spooned on top. Sprinkle with cheese.

Mezzani with Chicken Livers

TURKEY   Serves 4

This offering with the short name of *Ic* is long on flavor.

3 tablespoons of butter
3 tablespoons of olive oil
¼ cup of pignoli (pine nuts)
½ pound of chicken livers, coarsely
   chopped
¼ cup of black currants
3 cups of chicken broth

1 teaspoon of salt
½ teaspoon of pepper
½ pound of uncooked mezzani
   (medium-sized macaroni or
   maccheroni)
6 scallions (white part only), chopped
¼ cup of chopped fresh dill

In a saucepan, heat half of the butter and oil, and sauté the pignoli until golden; remove and set aside. In the same pan sauté the chicken livers for 2 minutes, or until they are cooked but still pink inside. In another pot, heat the remaining butter and oil, sauté the currants 1 minute; add the chicken broth, salt, and pepper. Bring to a boil and stir in the pasta; cook 5 minutes. Lower heat, cover, and cook for 10 minutes, or until the pasta is *al dente* and the broth is mainly absorbed. Stir in the pignoli, chicken livers, scallions, and dill. Taste for seasoning.

Spaghettini with Saged Chicken Livers

ITALY   Serves 4

We first has this simple but unusual dish in Calabria in a home on a cliff overlooking the sea.

6 tablespoons of butter
1 garlic clove, minced
1 pound of chicken livers, cleaned, then each liver quartered
Salt to taste
½ teaspoon of red-pepper flakes

3 thin slices of prosciutto (or other ham), slivered
1 teaspoon of chopped fresh sage
2 tablespoons of Marsala wine
½ pound of spaghettini, cooked *al dente*, drained

In a saucepan, melt the butter, add the garlic and livers, season with salt, and sprinkle on the red pepper. Stir in the ham and fresh sage. Cook, stirring, for 5 minutes. The livers should be browned, but pink inside. Do not overcook the livers, as they will become hard and unpalatable. Stir in the Marsala, blending well. Toss the sauce with the hot pasta and serve immediately.

Tagliolini with Chicken Livers and Veal Kidneys

SARDINIA   Serves 6 to 8

1 stick (¼ pound) of butter
2 garlic cloves, minced
1 pound of veal kidneys, cored, thinly sliced, and dusted lightly with flour
1 pound of chicken livers, cleaned and each quartered and dusted lightly with flour
Salt and pepper to taste

6 anchovy fillets, drained, minced
Juice of 1 lemon
½ teaspoon of dried basil
1 tablespoon of chopped broadleaf parsley
1 pound of tagliolini (narrow noodle), cooked *al dente*, drained

In a large saucepan, melt 2 tablespoons of butter and sauté the garlic for 1 minute. Add the remaining butter, and when it is bubbling, add the kidneys and cook for 2 minutes; add the livers, sprinkle with salt and pepper, stir in the anchovies, lemon juice, basil, and parsley, and cook, stirring, for 6 minutes, or until the kidneys and livers are brown on the outside but pink on the inside. Do not overcook. Taste for seasoning. Toss half of the kidney and liver sauce with the hot pasta. Spoon the remainder on top of individual servings.

Fettuccine with Sweetbreads and Ham

FRANCE   Serves 6

½ pound of sweetbreads
6 tablespoons of butter
¼ cup of dry vermouth
½ cup of diced, cooked ham
Pinch of dried thyme
Pinch of nutmeg

Salt and pepper to taste
1 cup of heavy cream
1 pound of fettuccine (a narrow
    noodle), cooked *al dente*, drained
1 cup freshly grated Gruyère cheese

Soak the sweetbreads for 1 hour in 4 cups of cold water and 1 tablespoon of white vinegar. Trim, removing the membranes. Place in a saucepan, and cover the sweetbreads with cold water. Bring to a boil, and simmer for 1 minute. Drain and cover with cold water. Remove any membranes you might have missed. Drain and dry sweetbreads with a towel. Cut them into cubes slightly larger than ½ inch. In a saucepan, melt 3 tablespoons of butter. Add the sweetbreads, and sauté over medium heat for 1 minute. Add the vermouth, and, over high heat, cook most of the wine off. Stir in the ham, thyme, nutmeg, salt, and pepper. Cook for 1 minute. Stir in the cream, and over low heat, simmer for 7 minutes. Taste for seasoning. Place the pasta in a warm bowl containing 3 tablespoons of soft butter. Mix well. Add one-third of the cheese. Toss well. Add one-third of the sauce. Toss well. Serve in hot rimmed soup bowls with the remaining sauce spooned on top. Pass the remaining cheese at the table.

Creamed Tagliatelle with Sweetbreads and Foie Gras

BELGIUM   Serves 6

4 tablespoons of butter
4 tablespoons of flour
3 cups of light cream
¼ cup of sherry
¼ teaspoon of nutmeg
Salt and pepper to taste
1 pound of tagliatelle (a narrow
   noodle), cooked very *al dente*,
   drained

1 two and three-fourths-ounce can
   of foie gras, diced
½ pound of cooked, diced sweetbreads
½ cup of grated Gruyère cheese
3 tablespoons of butter, melted
Paprika

In a saucepan, over low heat, melt the butter. Stir in the flour and cook, stirring, until you have a smooth paste. Gradually add the cream and cook, stirring, until you have a smooth, thickened sauce. Add the sherry, nutmeg, salt, and pepper. Place half of the noodles in the bottom of a buttered baking dish. Scatter the foie gras and sweetbreads over the noodles. Spoon half of the sauce in a layer over them. Make another layer of the remaining noodles and spoon over them the remaining sauce. Sprinkle with the cheese, dribble with butter, and sprinkle lightly with paprika. Place in a preheated 400-degree oven for 20 minutes or until it is golden.

Bavettine with Tripe

SWITZERLAND   Serves 4 to 6

Tripe and pasta may seem like an odd Swiss dish, but the country has great variety in food from one district to another. It is also surrounded by France, Italy, and Germany, and each country has influenced the cooking of Switzerland. This recipe borrows from both the French and the Italians.

3 tablespoons of olive oil
3 small white onions, chopped
2 garlic cloves, minced
2 pounds of honeycomb tripe, cubed
1 tablespoon of flour
1 teaspoon of salt
½ teaspoon of black pepper

1 cup of dry white wine
2 cups of chicken broth
1 cup of tomato purée
1 pound of bavettine (a thinner version of linguine), cooked *al dente*, drained

In a large pot, heat the oil and cook the onions and garlic until almost soft. Add the tripe and brown it; sprinkle with the flour, salt, black and red pepper. Stir in the wine and broth; cover and simmer for 2 hours. Stir in the tomato purée, and simmer, uncovered, for 30 minutes, or until the tripe is fork-tender (if sauce becomes too thick, add small amounts of hot broth). Taste for seasoning. Toss the hot pasta with half of the sauce; spoon the remainder on top of each serving.

VIII

Particular Pastas

(Cheese, Eggs, Butter, Etc.)

𝓕ETA CHEESE SAUCE, perciatelli soufflé, noodle kugel, tagliarini with the classic basil sauce, pesto, a Turkish rice-and-vermicelli pilaf, an Australian noodle pudding, a fantastic sauce with four world-famous cheeses, butter, and cream. Particular pastas indeed!

Particular people who watch their weight and control their appetite have discovered the same thing that we pointed out at the beginning of this book—pasta, in particular, is a valuable food both in terms of nutrition and weight control.

One of the world's foremost nutritionists, Ancel Keys, Professor Emeritus of Physiological Hygiene, University of Minnesota, says, "One of the least fattening cuisines in the world is the Italian cuisine: the real Italian cuisine consisting of a plate of pasta with tomato sauce, dressed with a little grated Parmesan, followed by a little meat or fish, a salad, and fresh fruit."

This is the perfect diet because when you eat pasta as a first course (no more than three ounces!), when you are hungriest, it quickly satisfies. Most of the particular pastas in this chapter will average no more than 425 calories for three ounces. As the average daily expenditure of energy for a woman is 2,500 calories, and a man, 3,000 calories, that dish of particular pasta is only about one-sixth of a normal woman's daily intake, and one-seventh of a man's.

If you want to make an entire meal of pasta (and why not?) and eat four or even five ounces, then you still have this complicated weight and calorie business under control—at less than 800 calories for a perfect meal.

Why these words on weight at this point? Because it is chapter VIII, we are nearing the end, and we want to reemphasize how "particular" pasta really is.

Ricciolini and Cheddar Loaf

UNITED STATES   Serves 6

2 tablespoons of butter
3 tablespoons of flour
1 cup of light cream
Salt and pepper to taste
½ pound of very sharp Cheddar
    cheese, grated

1 tablespoon of butter mixed with
    ½ teaspoon of garlic powder
¾ pound of ricciolini (little
    "curls"), cooked very *al dente*,
    drained
½ cup of coarse breadcrumbs

In a saucepan, melt the butter and add the flour, stirring until it is a smooth paste. Add the cream, a little at a time, stirring until smooth and thickened. Season to taste with salt and pepper. Add the cheese, stirring over medium heat until it melts. In a loaf pan, melt the garlic butter. Add the cooked pasta and the breadcrumbs to the cheese sauce, and blend. Spoon into the loaf pan; cook, uncovered, in a preheated 350-degree oven for 35 minutes, or until brown. Like most American pasta recipes, this is simple but tasty.

Eggs and Pennine

PORTUGAL   Serves 4

1 cup of light cream
¾ pound of pennine (small "pens," pasta tubes cut diagonally at both ends like a quill pen), cooked *al dente*, drained
1 cup of grated sharp cheese, Cheddar or Romano

⅛ teaspoon of mace
½ teaspoon of salt
½ teaspoon of pepper
4 hard-cooked eggs, cut into thick slices
2 tablespoons of butter

In a deep saucepan, bring the cream to a simmer, and stir in the pasta, three-fourths of the cheese, mace, salt, and pepper. Pour into a buttered baking dish, and place a layer of egg slices on top. Sprinkle with the remaining cheese and fleck with butter. Bake, uncovered, in a preheated 400-degree oven just until brown.

Spaghettini Frittata

ITALY   Serves 4

½ pound of spaghettini, broken into 1-inch pieces, cooked very *al dente*, drained
5 tablespoons of soft butter
¾ cup of grated Asiago or Parmesan cheese

4 eggs, beaten
3 tablespoons of chopped fresh parsley
Salt and pepper to taste
4 tablespoons of olive oil
1 medium-sized onion, minced

Mix the butter and half of the cheese with the pasta. Add the eggs, the remaining cheese, parsley, salt, and pepper. Mix well. Heat the olive oil in a large, heavy frypan. Add the onion and cook until soft. Stir in the spaghettini mixture, spreading it evenly. Lower heat, and cook about 5 minutes or until the bottom is set and golden; use a flexible spatula to loosen it and keep the frittata from sticking. Place a large plate over the frypan. Invert the frypan onto the plate so that the frittata rests on the plate, cooked side up. Slide it back into the frypan (cooked side up) and cook about 5 minutes, or until the other side of the frittata is set. Serve in wedges.

Ziti Rigati with Feta Cheese

GREECE   Serves 4 to 6

8 tablespoons of butter
1 pound of feta cheese, diced

1 pound of ziti rigati (elbow length), cooked *al dente*, drained
½ teaspoon of paprika

In a deep saucepan, melt the butter and sauté the cheese for 3 minutes. Stir in the pasta, sprinkle with the paprika. Make sure the cheese and butter are well blended with the pasta.

Fusilli with Gorgonzola Cheese and Pistachios

ITALY   Serves 4 to 6

1 stick of butter
¼ pound of Gorgonzola cheese, finely crumbled
¾ cup of medium cream
½ cup of skinned, finely ground pistachios

1 tablespoon of brandy
1 tablespoon of dry white wine
Salt and freshly milled black pepper to taste
1 pound of fusilli (twisted spaghetti), cooked *al dente*, drained

In a saucepan over low heat, melt the butter and cheese, stirring until they have blended. Stir in the cream, pistachios, brandy, white wine, salt (if necessary), and plenty of black pepper. Heat just to a simmer. Place the cooked pasta in a heated serving dish; cover with three-fourths of the sauce, and mix well. Spoon the remaining sauce evenly over the top.

Green Tagliarini with Four Cheeses

ITALY   Serves 4 to 6

¼ pound of butter
¼ pound of **Bel Paese cheese,** cut into
 small cubes
¼ pound of **Gorgonzola cheese,** cut
 into small cubes
¼ pound of **Fontina cheese,** cut into
 small cubes

½ cup of grated **Asiago or Parmesan
 cheese**
1 cup of **heavy cream**
 Freshly milled pepper
1 pound of **green tagliarini (a very
 narrow noodle),** cooked *al dente,*
 drained

In a large pot, over low heat, melt the butter; add the Bel Paese, Gorgonzola, and Fontina cheeses, stirring until melted. Stir in the Asiago (or Parmesan) cheese, and cream, blending well. Grind pepper liberally, into this hot cheese sauce. Using two forks, gently toss the cooked pasta with the sauce.

Macaroni and Cheese with Fresh Tomato Slices

UNITED STATES   Serves 6

2 tablespoons of butter
2 tablespoons of flour
1½ cups of light cream
Salt and pepper to taste
⅛ teaspoon of cayenne
2 cups of grated sharp Cheddar
cheese

1 pound of small elbow macaroni,
cooked very *al dente*, drained
3 large, ripe tomatoes, peeled and
each cut into 4 thick slices
⅔ cup of buttered breadcrumbs

In a saucepan, melt the butter and stir in the flour; continue stirring, over low heat, until butter and flour are a smooth paste. Gradually add the cream, stirring until the sauce is smooth and thickened. Season with salt, pepper, and cayenne. Add ½ cup of the cheese, and stir until melted. In a bowl, mix the cooked hot macaroni with the sauce, blending well. Spoon half of the sauced macaroni into a deep, buttered baking dish, then arrange 6 tomato slices over it; sprinkle liberally with cheese. Spoon in the remaining macaroni, then cover with the remaining tomato slices. Sprinkle with the remaining cheese, and cover with the breadcrumbs. Bake, uncovered, in a preheated 375-degree oven until bubbling and the top is brown and crusty.

Macaroni with Eggs (Macarron con Huevos)

MEXICO   Serves 6

4 tablespoons of butter
1 small onion, finely chopped
1 green chili, seeded, white ribs
removed, chopped
Salt and pepper to taste
2 cups of basic tomato sauce (see
page 144)

1½ cups of tubetti (a small tube pasta),
cooked very *al dente*, drained
6 eggs
½ to ¾ cup of freshly grated
Monterey Jack or Cheddar
cheese

In a saucepan, melt 2 tablespoons of butter, add the onion, the chili, salt and pepper; sauté until the vegetables are soft but not brown. Stir in the sauce, simmer for 3 minutes. Mix in the pasta. Spoon into a shallow, buttered baking dish and bake in a preheated 375-degree oven for 10 minutes. Make 6 depressions in the pasta and, with the remaining butter, dot the depressions. Break an egg into each. Sprinkle entire surface with the cheese. Return the dish to the oven and bake, uncovered, 10 minutes or until the eggs are cooked.

Baked Noodles

POLAND   Serves 4 to 6

1 pound of medium-broad egg
    noodles, cooked very *al dente*,
    drained
2 cups of sour cream
2 eggs, beaten
4 tablespoons of melted butter
½ teaspoon of salt
1 cup of grated Asiago or Parmesan
    cheese

Place the noodles in a buttered casserole, and mix the sour cream. Cook, in a preheated 200-degree oven, uncovered, until most of the sour cream has been absorbed by the noodles. Stir in the eggs, butter, and salt. Cover with the grated cheese and bake, uncovered, in a preheated 375-degree oven until the eggs have set and the top is brown.

Balkan Noodles

Serves 6

1 pound narrow egg noodles, cooked
    very *al dente*, drained
12 ounces of soft white farmer's cheese
2 small white onions, minced
1 pint sour cream
2 garlic cloves, minced
½ teaspoon of salt
1 teaspoon of minced fresh mint
½ teaspoon cayenne pepper

Blend the cheese, onions, sour cream, garlic, salt, mint, and cayenne, and toss with the cooked noodles. Bake in a buttered casserole, uncovered, in a preheated 350-degree oven for 30 minutes, or until bubbling and golden on top.

Caraway Noodle Ring

GERMANY   Serves 4

½ pound of ¼-inch-wide noodles,
    cooked very *al dente*, drained
4 tablespoons of butter
2 tablespoons of flour
1 cup of milk

1 tablespoon of caraway seeds
½ cup of grated Cheddar cheese
Salt to taste
Dash of cayenne pepper
3 eggs, well-beaten

Toss the cooked pasta with 2 tablespoons of butter. In a saucepan, over medium heat, melt the remaining butter. Add the flour; cook and stir into a smooth, golden paste. Add milk, a small amount at a time, cooking and stirring until the sauce is smooth. Stir in the caraway seeds and cheese, and cook over low heat, stirring until the cheese has melted. Stir in the cayenne, then season with salt. Cool slightly (so eggs won't curdle) then stir in the beaten eggs. Mix this sauce with the noodles, gently tossing with two forks. Spoon into a buttered 1½-quart ring mold. Set the mold in a pan of hot water, that reaches half way up on the mold; bake in a preheated 350-degree oven for 30 minutes or until the eggs set. Turn out on a hot plate, and fill the center with creamed chicken, creamed or curried shellfish, or creamed ham and sweetbreads with sherry.

Double Noodles Alsace

FRANCE   Serves 4

3 tablespoons of butter
½ pound of tagliolini (narrow
    noodles), cooked very *al dente*,
    drained

4 tablespoons of grated Gruyère
    cheese
Salt and pepper to taste
2 tablespoons of light olive oil

In a saucepan, melt the butter and stir in half of the noodles. Blend in the cheese, salt, and pepper; simmer for 3 minutes. Remove from stove and turn mixture into a heated serving dish. Meanwhile sauté the remaining noodles in the oil in a frypan until they are browned, but not too crisp. Ladle these noodles over those in the serving dish; serve in hot bowls.

Noodles and Cottage Cheese

RUSSIA   Serves 6

1 pound of fettuccine (a ¼-inch-wide
    noodle), cooked very *al dente*,
    drained
9 slices of bacon, cooked until
    crisp, crumbled
½ teaspoon of salt

2 cups of cottage cheese
2 eggs, beaten
½ cup of heavy cream
3 tablespoons of butter
½ cup of breadcrumbs

In a large bowl, place the noodles, crumbled bacon, and salt. Mix well, but gently. In another bowl, place cottage cheese, eggs, and cream; blend thoroughly. In a well-buttered baking dish or casserole, arrange a layer of the noodle and bacon mixture, cover with a layer of the cheese, egg, and cream mixture; repeat the layers, the last layer should be noodles. In a saucepan, melt the butter and stir in the breadcrumbs, blending well. Sprinkle a layer of the buttered crumbs over the noodles in the casserole. Bake, uncovered, in a preheated 350-degree oven for 25 minutes or until brown.

Noodle Kugel

JEWISH   Serves 6 to 8

This is usually served as an accompaniment for poultry.

1 pound of egg noodles, cooked very
   al dente, drained
5 tablespoons of sugar
8 tablespoons of sweet butter
5 eggs, beaten
1½ teaspoons of salt
½ cup of raisins, coarsely chopped

¾ cup of dried apricots, cut into
   ¼-inch pieces
3 medium-sized apples, peeled,
   cored, and cut into ¼-inch
   pieces
1 teaspoon of sugar   ⎫ blended
½ teaspoon of cinnamon ⎭

In a bowl, blend the noodles with the sugar, 7 tablespoons of butter, eggs, salt, raisins, apricots, and apples. With remaining butter coat a large casserole, and pour in the blended noodles. Sprinkle with the sugar-cinnamon blend and cook, uncovered, in the center of a preheated 350-degree oven for 40 minutes.

Noodle Pudding

AUSTRALIA   Serves 4

12 ounces of fine noodles, cooked very   1 onion, minced
    al dente, drained   1 garlic clove, minced
1 cup of sour cream   ½ teaspoon of salt
1 cup of small curd cottage cheese   ½ teaspoon of pepper
½ cup of medium cream   ½ cup of breadcrumbs
1 tablespoon of Worcestershire sauce   1 tablespoon of butter

In a bowl, combine the cooked pasta, sour cream, cottage cheese, cream, Worcestershire sauce, onion, garlic, salt, and pepper; blend well. Taste for seasoning. In a buttered baking dish, place the noodle mixture, sprinkle with breadcrumbs, fleck with butter. Cover, and cook in a preheated 350-degree oven for 20 minutes, or until brown and bubbling.

Noodles with Kasha

JEWISH   Serves 6

4 tablespoons of chicken fat (or   2 cups of chicken broth
    vegetable oil)   ½ pound of egg noodles, cooked
2 medium-sized onions, chopped   *al dente*, drained
1 cup of kasha (buckwheat groats)   3 tablespoons of butter
1 egg, beaten   Freshly milled black pepper
½ teaspoon of salt

In a deep frypan, melt the chicken fat (or heat the oil) and cook the onions until soft. Stir in the kasha, egg, and salt; add the chicken broth, cover the pan, bring to a boil, then lower the heat and simmer for 25 minutes. The broth should be absorbed and the kasha grains light and fluffy but separated. In a large heated bowl, place the kasha, noodles and butter; grind the pepper mill liberally over the top, and gently toss until well blended.

Tagliarini with Pesto Sauce

ITALY   Serves 6 to 8

This famous sauce, originating in Genoa, cannot be tampered with. It is a precise sauce. It must be made with fresh basil leaves, the fresher, the better. No substitutions are acceptable; no dried basil, no fresh spinach leaves. Thus, it is a summer sauce. It is also a favorite conversation piece wherever pasta lovers gather.

2 cups of fresh basil leaves, chopped
1 cup of chopped fresh broadleaf
   parsley
½ cup of grated Asiago cheese
½ cup of grated Romano cheese
1 tablespoon of pignoli (pine nuts)
12 walnuts, blanched, broken into
   pieces

12 almonds, blanched, halved
3 garlic cloves, quartered
  Salt to taste
4 tablespoons of butter
½ cup of olive oil
1½ pounds of tagliarini (thin noodles),
   cooked *al dente* (do not drain)

If you have a powerful blender or food processor, blend all ingredients except the pasta. If your blender is so-so, then blend in stages, a third of the basil leaves and parsley at a time. The purpose is to blend all the ingredients into a smooth green paste. In Genoa they use a mortar and pestle plus muscle and patience. Cook the pasta just before serving. Place the green pesto sauce in a hot bowl, then fork the pasta directly from its cooking water into the pesto paste. The water that remains on the strands of pasta is necessary to thin the sauce a bit and to aid in the blending. When well blended serve in warm dishes immediately. In the homes in Genoa it is served more elegantly. Hot pasta is placed on a plate, sprinkled with cheese, then centered with a very large spoonful of pesto sauce. That sauce is in a small pan on the stove, and just before serving, 2 tablespoons of hot water from the pasta pot are blended into the green sauce, perfectly thinning it to the right consistency.

Vermicelli and Rice Pilaf

TURKEY   Serves 6

Most of the Middle Eastern countries blend pasta with rice in interesting dishes, some with meat, fish, or poultry, some plain. Here is an excellent meatless pilaf that goes well with any stew-type dish.

1½ cups of rice	3 cups of chicken broth
½ tablespoon of salt	½ teaspoon of salt
1 stick (¼ pound) of butter	½ teaspoon of pepper
1 cup of broken-up vermicelli (in ¼-inch pieces)	8 scallions (white part only), chopped

In a bowl, place the rice and the ½ tablespoon of salt; cover with boiling water. Stir, cool, and drain. In a saucepan, melt 2 tablespoons of butter; lightly brown the pieces of vermicelli. Add the remaining butter, chicken broth, salt, and pepper. Bring to a boil, and cook for 2 minutes. Add the rice while the broth is still boiling; stir once. Cover and cook on high heat for 4 minutes. Lower to a simmer, and cook for 10 minutes, or until all the broth has been absorbed. Taste for seasoning. Stir in the scallions, remove from heat, cover with a cloth and then the pot cover; let set for 25 minutes. Gently reheat the pilaf when ready to serve. Fluff with a fork.

Spaetzle with Cheese and Onions

GERMANY   Serves 4 to 6

1 recipe of spaetzle, cooked and drained (page 11)	5 tablespoons of butter
2 medium-sized white onions, chopped	1 cup of grated Gruyère or Swiss cheese
	¼ cup of fine breadcrumbs

178

Cook the onions in 2 tablespoons of butter until soft, but not brown. Stir in the spaetzle. In a buttered baking dish arrange half of the spaetzle and onion mixture in a layer, sprinkle half of the cheese, then half of the bread-crumbs, and dot with half of the remaining butter. Repeat the layering, and bake in a preheated 375-degree oven for 30 minutes or until the top is golden.

Riccini Baked with Sour Cream

UNITED STATES   Serves 4 to 6

This small curl or twisted pasta is again a welcome sight-change from elbow macaroni.

1 pound of riccini (a short, twisted
    pasta), cooked very al dente,
    drained
4 tablespoons of melted butter

½ teaspoon of salt
¼ teaspoon of nutmeg
2 cups of sour cream
¾ cup of grated Monterey Jack cheese

In a bowl, place the hot pasta, add the butter, salt, and nutmeg; toss well. In a buttered casserole, arrange a thick layer of the pasta, form a well, and fill it with the sour cream. Sprinkle with the cheese and cook, uncovered, in a preheated 400-degree oven for 25 minutes, or until golden.

Noodles with Sour Cream and Cheese

GERMANY   Serves 4

½ **pound of broad noodles,** cooked
    very *al dente,* drained
4 tablespoons of butter, in small
    pieces
3 eggs, beaten

1 cup sour cream
½ **cup of grated Asiago or Parmesan**
    cheese
Salt to taste
½ **teaspoon of paprika**

Toss the cooked pasta with the butter. Combine the eggs, sour cream, cheese, and paprika. Blend well. Add salt to taste. Mix the egg, sour cream, and cheese mixture with the noodles. Spoon into a buttered baking dish and bake in a preheated 350-degree oven for 30 minutes, or until the eggs have set and the top begins to brown. This is good served with any meat or fowl roast.

Perciatelli Soufflé

NEW ZEALAND   Serves 4 to 6

1 cup of perciatelli (a hollow pasta,
    larger than spaghetti), broken
    into 1-inch pieces, cooked very
    al dente, drained
1 cup of grated very sharp aged
    Cheddar cheese
¼ **pound (1 stick) of butter,** softened
    but not melted

1 cup of light cream
3 eggs, separated
1 teaspoon of Worcestershire sauce
1 teaspoon of salt
½ **teaspoon of pepper**
⅛ **teaspoon of paprika**
¼ **teaspoon of dry mustard**
1 cup of breadcrumbs

Blend the cooked pasta with the cheese; set aside. In a bowl, blend the butter, cream, egg yolks, Worcestershire sauce, salt, pepper, paprika, and dry mustard. Place in a saucepan and heat (do not boil or the egg yolks will set). Place the breadcrumbs in a bowl and pour the egg yolk and cream, etc., mixture over them, letting it stand for 5 minutes or until the liquid is absorbed. Blend the cheese and pasta with the breadcrumbs mixture. Beat the egg whites until they are stiff and rising in peaks. Fold into the pasta and breadcrumbs mixture. Spoon into a buttered soufflé dish, and bake, uncovered, in a preheated 350-degree oven for 30 minutes or until set and golden on top.

Ziti al Forno

ITALY   Serves 4 to 6

This is the Italian pasta lover's favorite. *Al forno* simply means in the oven, baked.

1 pound of ziti (a large, long pasta tube), in 1-inch pieces, cooked very *al dente*, drained

3 tablespoons of butter, room temperature

1 teaspoon of black pepper

½ cup of grated Asiago or Parmesan cheese

½ cup of grated Romano cheese

1 pound of fresh ricotta cheese (about 1½ cups)

2 cups of Filetto Sauce (page 206)

In a bowl, place the ziti, butter, and pepper; toss well. Add half of the Asiago and the Romano; toss well. In a baking dish, make a layer of the pasta, sprinkle with Asiago and Romano, add a layer of ricotta, cover with sauce. Repeat the procedure until the pasta, cheeses, and sauce are used; the last layer should be sauce and grated cheese. Cook, uncovered, in a preheated 375-degree oven until bubbling and browned.

IX

Salads

*Q*UESTION, YOU WHO ARE PASTA FANS: How many of you have given serious thought to making salads from your favorite food?

We never had. But in travels that have taken us throughout Europe, the Near and Far East, among other places, we discovered that people everywhere thought that pasta was the perfect catalyst to convert an ordinary salad into an extraordinary one. We found dishes like a pasta-shell and crabmeat salad from Portugal, a Chinese cold bean sprouts and vermicelli salad, a pasta, cream, and roquefort salad from France. But read on. Convince yourself that salads need not be confined to lettuce and tomato.

Cold Rice Vermicelli and Bean Sprouts Salad

CHINA   Serves 8

1 tablespoon of peanut oil

2 eggs, beaten

4 cups of fresh bean sprouts, placed
    in a colander, 3 quarts of boiling
    water poured over them,
    drained and cooled

3 sweet, white cucumbers (canned),
    shredded

½ cup of chives, cut into 1-inch pieces

1 cup of shredded, roast pork

⅓ cup of light soy sauce

8 small hot green chilies in vinegar,
    or bottled Tabasco peppers,
    chopped

2 teaspoons of sesame oil

2 teaspoons of sugar

½ cup of white vinegar

1 tablespoon of chopped fresh ginger
    Salt to taste

3 ounces of rice vermicelli, placed in
    pot of boiling water, removed
    from heat, and allowed to set
    for 10 minutes; drained, rinsed
    under cold water, and drained
    again

In a saucepan, heat the oil and cook the eggs as for an omelet; cook until just set. Turn onto a plate, cool, then cut into 2-inch-long shreds and place in a large mixing bowl. Add the bean sprouts, cucumbers, chives, and pork to the eggs in the mixing bowl. In a saucepan, place the soy sauce, chilies, sesame oil, and sugar. Bring to a boil; set aside to cool. Blend the vinegar and ginger. Add ¼ cup of the vinegar mixture and 3 tablespoons of the soy sauce mixture to the bowl with the bean sprouts. Toss well and taste for seasoning, adding salt, if necessary. Serve the salad in individual salad plates on top of the noodles and pass the remaining sauce.

Farfalle Chef's Salad

UNITED STATES

Serves 6 to 8

½ cup of light cream
1 tablespoon of horseradish
½ cup of mayonnaise
2 tablespoons of wine vinegar
½ teaspoon of paprika
1 teaspoon of salt
½ teaspoon of pepper
2 cups of farfalle (small "butterflies,"
  or "bows"), cooked *al dente*,
  drained, and cooled
½ cup of julienne strips of smoked
  tongue
4 slices of boiled ham, cut into
  ⅛-inch strips

2 medium-sized ripe tomatoes,
  peeled, seeded, and quartered
6 medium-sized radishes, sliced
2 small cucumbers, peeled, seeded,
  and cut into thick slices
1 cup of bite-size pieces of Boston
  lettuce
1 cup of bite-size pieces of Romaine
  lettuce
1 cup of bite-size pieces of iceberg
  lettuce
2 hard-cooked eggs, quartered

In a large bowl, blend the cream, horseradish, mayonnaise, vinegar, paprika, salt, and pepper. Add the pasta and all of the remaining ingredients except the eggs. Toss well, thoroughly blending. Taste for seasoning. Garnish with the eggs.

Lumachine and Crabmeat Salad

PORTUGAL   Serves 6

1½ cups of lumachine (medium-sized
    pasta shells), cooked *al dente*,
    drained, and cooled
1 medium-sized green pepper,
    chopped (after removing seeds
    and white ribs)
1 pound of fresh, cooked crabmeat,
    picked over, flaked

1 tablespoon of capers, rinsed in
    water and drained
1 cup of mayonnaise mixed with
    2 tablespoons of lemon juice
Salt to taste
A good pinch of cayenne pepper
Boston lettuce leaves
2 pimentos cut into strips
2 hard-cooked eggs, quartered

Combine everything up to the lettuce leaves; mix thoroughly but gently.
Refrigerate until ready to serve. Line a bowl with the lettuce leaves. Spoon in
the pasta and crabmeat mixture, and garnish with the pimento strips and
hard-cooked eggs.

Pasta, Egg, and Salmon Salad

UNITED STATES   Serves 6

2 cups of small elbow macaroni,
    cooked *al dente*, drained, and
    cooled
1 seven and three-fourths-ounce can
    of red salmon, drained, flaked
3 tender celery ribs, scraped, finely
    chopped
4 hard-cooked eggs, chopped

1 teaspoon of salt
½ teaspoon of pepper
¾ cup of mayonnaise
½ teaspoon of Dijon mustard
6 large, crisp Boston lettuce leaves
6 stuffed green olives, halved
6 strips of pimento

In a bowl, thoroughly blend the pasta, salmon, celery, eggs, salt, pepper, mayonnaise, and mustard. Taste for seasoning. Chill. Place on lettuce leaves and top with the olives and pimento strips.

Maruzzine Salad with Fish

NORWAY   Serves 4 to 6

1 teaspoon of salt	2 celery ribs, scraped and chopped
½ teaspoon of pepper	½ of a pimento, chopped
1 tablespoon of white vinegar	2 cups of maruzzine (tiny pasta
3 tablespoons of olive oil	"shells"), cooked *al dente,*
1 teaspoon of finely chopped parsley	drained, and cooled
2 cups of diced, cooked fish	½ cup of mayonnaise
1 small white onion, minced	4 to 6 large, crisp lettuce leaves

In a salad bowl, place the pepper, vinegar, and half of the salt; blend well. Add the oil, stirring until the mixture is completely blended. Stir in the parsley. Add the fish, onion, celery, pimento, and the remaining salt. Blend and chill. In another bowl, mix the pasta shells with the mayonnaise, then carefully mix in the chilled fish mixture. Taste for seasoning. Serve on the lettuce leaves.

Rigatoni Garden Salad

ITALY   Serves 6 to 8

1 pound of rigatoni (large, grooved
   pasta tubes), cooked *al dente*,
   drained, and cooled
3 large, ripe tomatoes, peeled,
   seeded, chopped coarsely, and
   placed in a strainer over a bowl
   to drain

3 tablespoons of chopped fresh basil
6 tablespoons of olive oil
   Juice of 1 lemon
2 cloves of garlic, minced
1 teaspoon of salt
1 teaspoon of pepper

In a large bowl, combine the pasta and all other ingredients, tossing
well to blend. Taste for seasoning. This also can be lifted out of the salad
category by cooking the pasta at the last minute and serving the cold sauce
over the hot pasta.

Ditalini with Herring

SWEDEN   Serves 6 to 8

1 eight-ounce jar of herring "bits" in
   wine sauce, drained
6 scallions (white part only), finely
   chopped
6 medium-sized fresh beets, cooked,
   peeled, and cubed

2 cups of ditalini (small, short
   macaroni), cooked *al dente*,
   drained, and cooled
½ cup of heavy cream, whipped
Salt to taste

In a bowl, combine the herring (if the "bits" are large, dice them), scallions, and beets. Blend and chill for two hours. Add the ditalini, whipped
cream, and salt. Toss, blending thoroughly. Taste for seasoning.

Rotelle Salad with Lemon Dressing

NORTH AFRICA   Serves 4 to 6

3 medium-sized ripe tomatoes,
   peeled, seeded, and cubed or
   coarsely chopped
6 scallions (white part only),
   coarsely chopped
1 medium-sized cucumber, peeled,
   quartered lengthwise, seeds
   removed, and coarsely chopped
1 medium-sized red pepper, seeded,
   white ribs removed, and
   chopped
Grated peel of 2 lemons
¼ cup of lemon juice

1½ teaspoons of salt
⅛ teaspoon of Tabasco sauce
⅔ cup of olive oil
2 garlic cloves, minced
½ teaspoon of paprika
1 teaspoon of sugar
¼ teaspoon of ground cumin
¼ teaspoon of coriander
¼ teaspoon of dry mustard
2 cups of rotelle (small pasta
   "wheels"), cooked *al dente*,
   drained, cooled

In a bowl, place the tomatoes, scallions, cucumber, and pepper. Chill. In a blender or food processor combine the grated lemon peel, lemon juice, salt, Tabasco, olive oil, garlic, paprika, sugar, cumin, coriander, and mustard. Blend until well mixed. Chill. Pour the sauce into the bowl with the vegetables, tossing to mix well. Use the pasta as a bed upon which to serve the sauced vegetables.

Farfallette and Meat (or Poultry) Salad

BELGIUM   Serves 6

1½ cups of farfallette (small pasta
  "butterflies"), cooked *al*
  dente, drained and cooled
2½ cups of cooked, cooled meat or
  poultry, cut into small cubes
1 tender celery rib, scraped and
  chopped
18 pitted black olives
3 tablespoons of wine vinegar or
  lemon juice

6 tablespoons of olive oil
1 teaspoon of salt
  Black pepper to taste
½ teaspoon of mustard (Dijon or
  some other good mustard)
1 garlic clove, finely minced
  Boston lettuce leaves
1 tablespoon of finely chopped
  parsley

Combine the pasta, meat or poultry, celery, and olives in a bowl.
Refrigerate. Combine the vinegar or lemon juice, olive oil, salt, pepper,
mustard, and garlic, and blend thoroughly. When ready to serve add this
salad dressing to the pasta and meat bowl; mix well but gently. Taste for
seasoning. Line a salad bowl with the lettuce leaves. Spoon in the salad, and
garnish with the parsley.

Danish Macaroni Salad

This is a Copenhagen favorite, often served with marvelous draft beer in the better bars.

Serves 4

1 medium-sized cucumber, peeled, halved, seeded, and cut into ½-inch pieces

4 ounces of maruzzine (small pasta shells), cooked *al dente*, well drained, and cooled

3 pickled herring filets, cut into ½-inch slices

4 scallions, white part only, coarsely chopped

4 small fresh mushrooms, thinly sliced

2 tablespoons of wine vinegar ⎤
2 tablespoons of olive oil ⎬ blended
1 teaspoon of salt ⎦

2 teaspoons of curry powder

1 cup of sour cream

In a salad bowl, place the cucumber, pasta shells, herring, scallions and mushrooms. Pour in the vinegar-oil-salt blend and mix well but gently. Refrigerate for 2 hours. Just before serving, blend the curry and sour cream, pour over the salad and mix well.

Reginini Summer Salad with Roquefort Cream

FRANCE   Serves 4

1½ cups of reginini ("little queens," small, short pasta tubes), cooked *al dente*, drained, and cooled
1 seven-ounce can of tuna, drained, and flaked
1 hard-cooked egg, chopped
6 pitted black olives, sliced
6 radishes, sliced
½ teaspoon of salt

1 small green pepper, seeded, white ribs removed, and chopped
½ cup of heavy cream, whipped
3 walnut-sized pieces of Roquefort cheese, crumbled
1 cup of mayonnaise
4 large crisp Boston lettuce leaves
2 ripe tomatoes, peeled, seeded, quartered

In a large bowl, place the pasta, tuna, egg, olives, radishes, salt, and pepper. Chill. Fold the whipped cream and cheese into the mayonnaise and add it to the pasta and tuna bowl; toss lightly to blend. Taste for seasoning. Serve on lettuce leaves garnished with tomato wedges.

Macaroni and Sardine Salad

NORWAY   Serves 4 to 6

2 cups of seeded, diced cucumbers
2 small white onions, diced
½ cup of white vinegar
3 tablespoons of clam broth
¼ cup of sugar
1 teaspoon of salt
½ teaspoon of pepper

2 cups of elbow macaroni, cooked *al dente*, drained and cooled
1 cup of sour cream
1 three and a half-ounce can of Norwegian brisling sardines, drained

In a bowl, combine the cucumbers, onions, vinegar, clam broth, sugar, salt, and pepper. Mix, then chill for 2 hours. Drain. Add the macaroni, sour cream, and sardines to the cucumber bowl. Toss well to blend. Taste for seasoning. This is a hot weather dish best served very cold.

Pennine and Scallops Salad

UNITED STATES   Serves 6 to ċ

1 pound of bay scallops
2 cups of dry white wine
2 cups of pennine (small "pens" or "feathers"), cooked *al dente*, drained, and cooled
1 tender celery rib, scraped, diced
2 tablespoons of minced white onion
½ teaspoon of salt

¼ teaspoon of dry mustard
¼ teaspoon of dill weed
1 tablespoon of horseradish
¼ cup of chili sauce
½ pint of sour cream
Crisp bibb or Boston lettuce leaves
2 tablespoons of chopped fresh dill

In a saucepan, over medium heat, simmer the scallops in the wine, for 10 minutes, or until firm but still tender. Do not overcook. Drain and cool. In a bowl combine the pasta, scallops, celery, and onion. Blend well. Chill. In another bowl, thoroughly mix the salt, mustard, dill weed, horseradish, chili sauce, and sour cream. Gently mix this into the pasta mixture, tossing to blend. Taste for seasoning. Serve spooned on the lettuce leaves. Garnish with fresh dill.

Shell Salad

UNITED STATES   Serves 4

Vary the usual elbow macaroni by using maruzzelle, "small seashells," for eye-appeal.

2 cups of cooked shells
2 tablespoons of fresh lemon juice
1 tablespoon of peanut oil
1 medium-sized white onion, minced
1 tablespoon of chopped chives
1 tablespoon of chopped broadleaf
    parsley

1 cup of diced celery (scrape the celery
    ribs before dicing)
12 chopped stuffed green olives
Salt and pepper to taste
2 tablespoons of sour cream
2 tablespoons of chopped pimento

Mix the pasta with lemon juice and oil. Chill for 2 hours. Blend in the onion, chives, parsley, celery, olives, salt, pepper, sour cream, and pimento.

Ditali and Shrimp Salad

UNITED STATES   Serves 6

1½ cups of ditali (macaroni cut in short
    lengths), cooked *al dente*,
    drained, and cooled
¾ pound of cooked, cleaned,
    medium-sized or small shrimp
    (if medium-sized are used,
    cut them in half)
4 scallions, finely chopped

1 cup of mayonnaise mixed with
    ½ teaspoon of curry powder
Juice of ½ a lemon
Pinch of ginger
Salt to taste
Boston lettuce leaves
2 tablespoons of finely chopped
    chives

Combine all ingredients except the lettuce leaves and chives; mix thoroughly but gently. Refrigerate until ready to serve. Line a bowl with the lettuce and spoon in the pasta and shrimp mixture. Sprinkle the top with the chives and serve.

Maccheroncelli and Tuna Salad

ITALY   Serves 6 to 8

2 garlic cloves, crushed
3 anchovy fillets
3 fresh basil leaves
3 tablespoons of chopped broadleaf
    parsley
8 tablespoons of olive oil
6 tablespoons of lemon juice
½ teaspoon of cayenne pepper
1 teaspoon of salt
½ teaspoon of black pepper

1 pound of maccheroncelli (small
    elbow macaroni), cooked *al
    dente,* drained, and cooled
½ cup of pitted, sliced black olives
1 seven-ounce can of tuna (Italian,
    in olive oil), drained, and
    flaked
¼ pound of Fontina cheese, cut
    julienne style

On a chopping board (or in a food processor) mince together into a paste the garlic, anchovies, basil and parsley. In a salad bowl, place the olive oil and lemon juice; blend well. Stir in the garlic and anchovy paste, the cayenne pepper, salt, and black pepper. Blend in the pasta, olives, tuna, and cheese. Taste for seasoning.

CARAWAY SEEDS

X

Vegetables

*W*E'VE ALWAYS BEEN OF THE OPINION that the last chapter of any book should be the best. Proof that the author or authors have not run out of steam.

This chapter, we hope, will leave you with that feeling. For there is no greater proof of pasta's versatility and economy than the magic it makes with vegetables: mating small pasta shells and cauliflower with eggs and cream, noodles with cabbage, pairing broccoli with pasta and anchovies, spaetzle with sauerkraut, fettuccelle with peas.

But there is no end to what you can do with pasta. The peoples of the world have always known that. A single book such as this can barely touch their accumulated knowledge.

Dushinar (Baked Spaghetti)

IRAN   Serves 6

1 **pound of spaghetti**, broken into
    2-inch pieces, cooked very *al*
    dente, and drained
4 **tablespoons of butter**
8 **tomatoes**, sliced
4 **eggs**

2 **cups of sour cream**
1 **cup light cream**
  Salt to taste
2 **teaspoons of cayenne pepper**
2 **tablespoons of ground walnuts**

Toss the pasta in 2 tablespoons of the butter. Butter a 12-inch casserole
and arrange a layer of spaghetti, then one layer of tomato slices, and continue,
finishing with a layer of pasta. Beat the eggs, blend with the sour cream and
sweet cream, and salt; beat together for 3 minutes. Pour over the spaghetti.
Blend cayenne and walnuts, and sprinkle over the top. Fleck with the remaining butter and bake, uncovered, in a preheated 375-degree oven for 30 minutes, or until bubbling and brown on top.

Fried Soba (Buckwheat or Spinach) Noodles with Cabbage

JAPAN   Serves 4

1 **cup of cut-up Chinese cabbage**,
    in ½-inch squares
4 **tablespoons of peanut oil**
1 **pound of** *soba* **noodles**, cooked
    soft, drained
6 **teaspoons of soy sauce**

½ **teaspoon of togarashi** (an
    authoritative mixture of crushed
    red pepper and other
    seasonings)
6 **scallions**, cut into ½-inch lengths

In a deep saucepan, heat the oil, and cook the cabbage 2 minutes. Do not overcook. Add the noodles, soy sauce, and togarashi; toss to blend. Serve very hot garnished with the scallions.

Lingue di Passeri with Broccoli, Anchovies, and Pignoli

ITALY   Serves 4 to 6

⅔ bunch (about 1 pound) of broccoli (select broccoli with dark green, tight buds)

½ cup of olive oil

1 two-ounce can of flat anchovies, drained

2 large garlic cloves, minced

½ cup of pignoli (pine nuts) sautéed in 2 tablespoons of butter until golden and crisp

1 pound of lingue di passeri (a flat spaghetti, larger than linguine), cooked *al dente,* and drained

Pepper to taste

Cut and divide the flowerets from the broccoli stalks (use the stalks for something else). Cook the flowerets in boiling, salted water for 2 minutes, or until tender but crunchy (do not overcook, they are better underdone than overdone). Set aside. In a frypan, heat the olive oil, add the anchovies and garlic; over low heat, cook, stirring, until the anchovies have disintegrated. Stir the broccoli into the anchovy sauce. Place the cooked pasta into a hot deep dish. Grind the pepper over it. Spoon one-third of the sauce over it; toss carefully. Spoon the remaining sauce over the top, then sprinkle with the crisp pignoli. Serve immediately.

Noodles with Sautéed Cabbage

HUNGARY   Serves 6

1 medium-sized head of cabbage,
    finely shredded
1 tablespoon of salt
1½ sticks of butter (12 tablespoons)
2 small white onions, minced

2 teaspoons of sugar
1 teaspoon of pepper
1 pound of egg noodles, cooked
    al dente, drained

In a bowl, place the shredded cabbage and salt; mix well and let set for 3 hours. Rinse with cold water, drain, and dry. In a pot, melt half of the butter. Add the onions, and cook until soft. Add the cabbage, sugar, and pepper. Cover and cook over low heat for 1 hour; stir often. Add the remaining butter, mixing it in well, and cook for 20 minutes. Add the noodles, blending them with the cabbage; cook for 10 minutes. Taste for seasoning.

Maruzzine with Cauliflower

FINLAND   Serves 4 to 6

1 medium-sized head of cauliflower,
    separated into flowerets
1 cup of maruzzine (small pasta
    shells), cooked very *al dente*,
    drained

3 eggs, beaten
1 cup of light cream
Salt to taste
Dash of mace

In a pot of boiling salted water, cook the cauliflower for 15 minutes, or until tender yet still crisp. Arrange it in a well-buttered casserole in one layer. In a bowl, blend the pasta, eggs, cream, salt, and mace. Pour this over the cauliflower. Bake, uncovered, in a preheated 350-degree oven for 30 minutes, or until the custard has set.

Cold Ziti with Cauliflower

ITALY   Serves 6 to 8

8 tablespoons of pesto (page 176)   ½ teaspoon of hot red-pepper flakes
2 tablespoons of olive oil   1 pound of ziti (large tube pasta),
2 garlic cloves, minced   cooked *al dente*, drained
1 medium-sized head of cauliflower,   2 medium-sized very ripe fresh
    divided into flowerets, cooked   tomatoes, skinned, seeded, and
    al dente (crisp but tender) in   cut into bite-sized pieces
    salted water, drained   Salt and pepper to taste

Prepare the pesto, set aside. In a saucepan, heat the oil, and sauté the garlic until soft; be careful not to burn it. Stir in the cooked cauliflower, sprinkle with the red pepper; cook, stirring gently, to heat through and blend. Set aside. In a bowl, place the cooked ziti, stir in the pesto, add the cauliflower and the tomato, salt, and pepper; blend well. Do not refrigerate, serve at room temperature.

Funghini with Celery Root

BULGARIA   Serves 4

All over Europe the various forms of Italian pasta are used in original recipes of the country. What shape pasta is used depends upon the fancy of the cook. This one we had in the home of a Bulgarian friend.

4 tablespoons of fat (Bulgarians use   1 tablespoon of tomato paste
    rendered pork fat, but butter is   ½ teaspoon of salt
    also excellent)   ½ teaspoon of pepper
1 large celery root, peeled, cut into 1 tablespoon of chopped broadleaf
    small cubes   parsley
½ cup of funghini (small   2 cups of boiling chicken broth
    "mushrooms"), or any small   ½ cup of grated Asiago or Parmesan
    soup pasta of your choice   cheese

In a saucepan, heat the pork fat or butter and sauté the celery root until nearly soft. Stir in the pasta; cook for 5 minutes. Add the tomato paste, salt, pepper, parsley, and chicken broth. Simmer, stirring for 10 minutes, until pasta is cooked *al dente*. Taste for seasoning. Sprinkle with cheese and serve.

Fedelini with Filetto Sauce

ITALY   Makes about 6 cups of sauce (some for the freezer);
                                     the pasta will serve 6

This is a special light sauce that restaurateurs in Italy make on Sundays and serve to themselves and their staffs on fresh pasta that day. It is a special sauce for us, too, to which we often add other ingredients when we wish to vary it. It freezes well, thus we usually make up a big batch. Its creators use prosciutto fat to sauté the onions and garlic, but we've found that olive oil does the job nicely.

4 tablespoons of olive oil
4 garlic cloves, minced
4 large onions, finely chopped
1½ teaspoons of salt
½ teaspoon of pepper
2 teaspoons of dry oregano
2 tablespoons of dry basil
⅛ teaspoon of hot red-pepper flakes

3 pounds of very ripe plum tomatoes, peeled, seeded and chopped, or 2 two-pound cans of Italian plum tomatoes (with basil), run through a food mill
½ teaspoon of sugar
1 pound of fedelini (one of the thinnest of spaghettis), cooked *al dente*, drained
A good grated cheese of your choice; we recommend Asiago

In a pot, heat the oil, and sauté the garlic until soft. Add the onions and cook until soft. Stir in the salt, pepper, oregano, basil, and red-pepper flakes, blending well. Add the tomatoes and sugar, stirring them into the other ingredients until well mixed. Bring to a boil, then lower to a simmer and cook, uncovered, for about 35 minutes, stirring often. The appeal of this sauce is its lightness, so do not overcook. When you can move a wooden spoon across the top of the sauce without leaving a watery trail, it is ready. It should be smooth and thick but not heavy. Do not revert to other pasta sauce techniques and use either tomato paste or the "crushed tomatoes" that come in a can. This destroys the personality of Filetto Sauce.

Toss at least a cup of the sauce with the hot cooked pasta. Spoon generous amounts over individual servings and freeze the rest. Pass the cheese of your choice at the table.

Small Elbows with Green Pepper Sauce

TURKEY   Serves 4

3 medium-sized green peppers, seeds
    and white part removed,
    and coarsely chopped
½ cup of olive oil
¼ cup of lemon juice

1 teaspoon of dry mustard
1 teaspoon of salt
½ teaspoon of pepper
½ pound of small elbow macaroni,
    cooked *al dente*, drained

The sauce should be prepared and refrigerated overnight, then let set at room temperature for 2 hours just before serving. In a bowl, place the peppers, oil, lemon juice, mustard, salt, and pepper. Blend well. Before serving, taste for seasoning. The pasta should be very hot and tossed well with the sauce. This dish is often used to accompany a simple meat course instead of rice or potatoes.

Nocciole with Kasha and Peas

CZECHOSLOVAKIA   Serves 4 to 6

1½ cups of *kasha* (coarse buckwheat
     groats)
  1 egg, beaten
  4 cups of beef broth
  ½ teaspoon of salt
  5 tablespoons of butter, room
     temperature

1½ cups of nocciole (a shell pasta,
     meaning "hazelnut"), cooked
     al dente, drained and tossed
     with 1 tablespoon of melted
     butter and a liberal milling of
     black pepper
  1 cup of tiny, sweet fresh cooked
     peas

In a frypan, place the kasha, and stir in the egg. Over low heat, stirring, blend well, coating the kasha with the egg. Add the beef broth and the salt; cover and simmer for 25 minutes, or until the kasha is tender and all of the broth is absorbed. Add the butter and toss, blending it with the hot kasha. Add the pasta and the peas to the kasha and toss. Taste for seasoning.

Baked Macaroni and Mushrooms

SWEDEN   Serves 6

  3 tablespoons of butter
  1 large white onion, finely chopped
  1 pound of fresh mushrooms,
     coarsely chopped
 12 ounces of elbow macaroni, cooked
     al dente, drained

  2 cups of medium cream
  2 eggs, beaten
1½ teaspoons of salt
  ½ teaspoon of pepper
  ½ cup of breadcrumbs

In a saucepan, melt the butter, and cook the onion until soft. Add the mushrooms, and cook for 4 minutes. In a buttered casserole or baking dish, evenly spread a layer of half of the macaroni. Sprinkle the onions and mushrooms evenly on top, and cover with a layer of the remaining macaroni. In a bowl, blend the cream, eggs, salt, and pepper; pour over the macaroni. Sprinkle the top with breadcrumbs; bake, uncovered, in a preheated 350-degree oven for 25 minutes, or until the custard has set and the top is golden.

Phat Wun Sen (Mixed Fried Vermicelli)

THAILAND   Serves 6

When we asked for recommendations for a noodle dish in Bangkok, this was always suggested. "Mixed" was certainly an apt description. Like many Asian dishes, this looks like a mess but tastes marvelous.

2 **tablespoons of peanut oil**
4 **garlic cloves,** minced
2 **fresh red chilies,** seeded, sliced
    diagonally
½ **pound of lean pork,** shredded
½ **pound of shrimp,** shelled, deveined
8 **scallions,** cut into ¼-inch pieces
2 **canned bamboo shoots,** cut julienne
    style
3 **small carrots,** cut julienne style

12 **dried small black Chinese mushrooms,** soaked in hot water for 20 minutes; water squeezed out, stems discarded, thinly sliced
2 **tablespoons of fish sauce**
1 **tablespoon of white vinegar**
1 **teaspoon of salt**   } blended
½ **teaspoon of pepper**
2 **teaspoons of sugar**
1 **pound of rice vermicelli,** soaked in hot water for 10 minutes, then well drained

In a wok, or large frypan, heat the oil over medium heat and cook the garlic and chilies until soft. Add the pork; cook for 8 minutes, stir-frying. Stir in the shrimps, scallions, bamboo shoots, carrots, and mushrooms; stir-fry for 5 minutes. Add the fish sauce, blended seasonings, and the vermicelli; mix well and cook for 2 minutes, or until it is heated through.

Vermicelli with Mushroom Sauce

PARAGUAY   Serves 4 to 6

2 tablespoons of olive oil
2 medium-sized white onions, chopped
2 chorizo sausages, poached in water, skinned, and thinly sliced
¼ pound of cured ham, cut julienne style
1 cup of Filetto Sauce (page 206)
3 slices of lean bacon, chopped

½ teaspoon of salt
½ teaspoon of pepper
1 cup of fresh chopped mushrooms
1 cup of chicken broth
¾ pound of vermicelli, cooked very *al dente*, drained
1 cup of grated Asiago or Parmesan cheese

In a saucepan, heat the oil. Add the onions and sausage slices; sauté for 10 minutes. Stir in the ham, tomato sauce, bacon, salt, and pepper. Cover, and simmer for 20 minutes. Stir in the mushrooms and chicken broth; simmer, uncovered, for 10 minutes. Taste for seasoning. In a buttered baking dish, alternate layers of pasta and sauce; sprinkle each with cheese. Bake uncovered in a preheated 375-degree oven for 20 minutes, or until brown and bubbling.

Noodles Baked with Fresh Mushrooms

POLAND   Serves 4

6 tablespoons of butter
1 pound of fresh mushrooms, thinly
    sliced
Salt and pepper to taste

1 tablespoon of chopped broadleaf
    parsley
½ pound of noodles, cooked very *al
    dente*, drained
3 tablespoons of fine breadcrumbs

In a saucepan, melt 4 tablespoons of the butter, and sauté the mushrooms for 6 minutes. Season with salt and pepper; stir in the parsley. Butter a casserole; alternate layers of mushrooms and noodles, ending with noodles. Sprinkle with breadcrumbs, fleck with the remaining butter; bake, uncovered, in a preheated 375-degree oven for 15 minutes, or until golden.

Noodles and Spinach

UKRAINE   Serves 6

1 pound of broad noodles, cooked
    very *al dente*, drained
4 tablespoons of butter, melted
1 cup of grated Romano cheese
4 tablespoons of butter
4 medium-sized white onions,
    chopped

2 pounds of fresh spinach, cooked,
    drained, and chopped
Salt and pepper to taste
½ cup of breadcrumbs
3 hard-cooked eggs, quartered

In a large bowl, toss the cooked noodles with the melted butter and half of the cheese. In a saucepan, melt 2 tablespoons of butter and cook the onions until soft; stir in the spinach and cook over high heat until all moisture has evaporated. Season with salt and pepper. In a well-buttered baking dish or casserole, arrange one-third of the noodles in an even layer, and cover with half of the spinach; repeat layers, ending with the noodles. In a saucepan, melt the remaining 2 tablespoons of butter and, off heat, stir in the bread-crumbs and the remaining cheese. Sprinkle this evenly over the noodles; bake, uncovered, in a preheated 375-degree oven for 25 minutes, or until the top is brown. Serve from the casserole garnished with the eggs.

Onion Sauce for German Ravioli*

To make 2 cups

3 tablespoons of butter
3 medium-sized onions, finely
    chopped
2 tablespoons of flour

2½ cups of rich beef broth
½ teaspoon of celery salt
Pepper to taste

In a frypan, melt the butter, cook the onions until soft. Add the flour, stirring constantly, until you have a smooth paste. Gradually add the beef broth, stirring constantly into a medium sauce. Stir in the celery salt. Season to taste with the pepper. Add the ravioli to the sauce; gently heat through.

* See page 101 for recipe for German ravioli.

Margherita with Peas and Ham

ITALY   Serves 6

This one depends upon swiftness; have everything ready, then work fast in the mixing and serving.

1 stick (¼ pound) of butter, room temperature, cut into thin slices
Fresh ground black pepper
1 pound of margherita (a narrow noodle, rippled along one side)
1 cup of grated Asiago or Parmesan cheese

⅓ cup of heavy cream, hot
1 cup of tiny sweet fresh peas, cooked *al dente*, drained
½ cup of shredded ham, preferably prosciutto
Salt to taste

Place the butter in a hot bowl, liberally grind the pepper mill over the butter; keep the bowl warm as you cook the pasta *al dente*. Fork the pasta out directly from the cooking pot; shake off excess water. Add pasta to the butter bowl; toss. Immediately add the cheese, cream, peas, salt, and ham; toss well and serve immediately on hot plates.

Penne and Peppers

MEXICO   Serves 4 to 6

1 pound of penne (short pasta tubes cut diagonally on both ends), cooked very *al dente*, drained
1 cup of heavy cream ⎫
4 large poblano chilies (or bell peppers), toasted ⎬ blended
skinned, seeded, ground ⎪
Salt and pepper to taste ⎭

5 tablespoons of butter
1 medium-sized white onion, chopped
½ cup of grated Asiago or Parmesan cheese

Cook the pasta, prepare the pepper sauce, and set aside. In a deep sauce-pan, melt 3 tablespoons of butter and cook the onion until soft. Stir in the pasta. With remaining butter, grease a casserole and arrange alternating layers of pasta, chili (or pepper) sauce, and cheese. Cook, uncovered, in a preheated 350-degree oven for 25 minutes or until brown and bubbling.

Neapolitan Peppers Stuffed with Perciatelli

ITALY   Serves 6

6 large firm green peppers
1 garlic clove, minced
3 tablespoons of olive oil
1 one-pound can of Italian plum
   tomatoes, chopped
½ teaspoon of dried basil
6 large black olives, chopped
4 anchovy fillets, chopped

1 tablespoon of capers, rinsed and
   dried
¼ teaspoon of oregano
Pepper to taste
Salt
½ pound of perciatelli (a long, hollow
   pasta), broken up, cooked very
   al dente, and drained
1 cup of beef broth

Cut the tops off the peppers and reserve them; scoop out the seeds and white part. In a saucepan, sauté the garlic in the olive oil until golden. Stir in the tomatoes and basil and simmer 20 minutes or until the sauce has thickened. Stir in the olives, anchovies, capers, oregano, and pepper. Mix the cooked pasta with the sauce. Very lightly salt the inside of the peppers. Fill them with the pasta mixture. Replace the tops of the peppers. Arrange them in a casserole just large enough to hold them. Pour in about ½ inch of broth to cover the bottom of the pan. Bake in a preheated 350-degree oven, covered; bast with the broth, and cook for 30 minutes, or until the peppers are tender. If the liquid cooks off, add a small amount of hot water.

Fides (or Vermicelli) and Rice Pilaf with Mushrooms

GREECE   Serves 6

5 tablespoons of butter
1 medium-sized white onion,
   chopped
1 cup of fides (or vermicelli), finely
   broken up

1 cup of rice
2½ cups of hot chicken broth
½ pound of small fresh mushrooms,
   thinly sliced
Salt and pepper to taste

In a saucepan that has a tight-fitting cover, melt 3 tablespoons of butter. Add the onion and cook until the onion is soft. Add the fides and rice; stir until they are coated with butter. Stir in the hot broth, cover, and simmer over low heat for 20 minutes. Remove from the heat and let set, covered, for 10 minutes. Meanwhile in a frypan, sauté the mushrooms in the remaining 2 tablespoons of butter until they are tender but still quite firm. Season with salt and pepper. Fluff the rice and fides with a fork. Then, still using a fork, mix in the mushrooms and their liquid. Taste for seasoning and serve immediately.

Spaetzle with Winekraut

GERMANY   Serves 6 to 8

4 tablespoons of butter
1 pound of fresh or canned
    sauerkraut, rinsed and drained
½ tablespoon of caraway seeds

½ cup of beef broth
1 cup of dry white wine
Salt and pepper to taste
1 basic recipe of spaetzle (see page 11)

In a heavy casserole, heat two tablespoons of butter. Add the sauerkraut, cover tightly, and simmer for half an hour, stirring from time to time. Add the caraway seeds, broth, wine, salt, and pepper; continue to simmer, covered, until sauerkraut is tender and the liquid has cooked off. Meanwhile, cook the spaetzle, drain, and toss with the remaining butter. Combine the spaetzle with the sauerkraut and serve.

Pappardelle with Tomato-Garlic Sauce

ITALY   Serves 6

10 garlic cloves, minced
 4 tablespoons of olive oil
½ teaspoon of dried basil
  Salt and pepper to taste
 2 tablespoons of Marsala wine
½ cup of dry red wine
 3 cups of Filetto Sauce (page 206)

3 tablespoons of chopped parsley
1 pound of pappardelle (a broad
   noodle), cooked *al dente*,
   drained
3 tablespoons of butter
1 cup grated Asiago or Parmesan
  cheese

In a heavy frypan, sauté the garlic in the oil until it begins to turn color (do not brown it). Stir in the basil, salt, pepper, Marsala, red wine, and Filetto Sauce. Simmer for 5 minutes. Stir in the parsley. Place the pasta in a hot bowl with the butter. Mix in half of the sauce and half of the cheese. Toss well. Serve in hot rimmed soup bowls with the remaining sauce spooned over. Pass the remaining cheese at the table.

Lumache with Vegetable Sauce

YUGOSLAVIA   Serves 4 to 6

1 stick (¼ pound) of butter
2 red peppers, seeds and white ribs removed, cut into 1½-inch strips
2 medium-sized white onions, minced
2 garlic cloves, minced
4 small zucchini, not peeled, cut into ¼-inch slices
1 cup of tender, sweet fresh peas
5 large basil leaves, minced
Salt and pepper to taste
1 pound of lumache ("snail"-shaped pasta), cooked *al dente*, drained
3 eggs, beaten
½ cup of grated Asiago or Parmesan cheese
2 tablespoons of minced broadleaf parsley

In a saucepan, melt the butter, and add the peppers, onions, garlic, zucchini, peas, and basil. Season with salt and pepper; sauté for 10 minutes, or until the vegetables are tender but still somewhat crisp. In a heated bowl, place the cooked, drained pasta (it must be very hot), toss well, but carefully, with the beaten eggs. Add the cooked vegetables, the grated cheese and the parsley; toss to blend.

INDEX